WRITINGS ON PSYCHOANALYSIS

EUROPEAN PERSPECTIVES

EUROPEAN PERSPECTIVES

A Series in Social Thought and Cultural Criticism

Lawrence D. Kritzman, Editor

European Perspectives presents English translations of books by leading European thinkers. With both classic and outstanding contemporary works, the series aims to shape the major intellectual controversies of our day and to facilitate the tasks of historical understanding.

LOUIS ALTHUSSER

WRITINGS ON PSYCHOANALYSIS

Freud and Lacan

EDITED BY

Olivier Corpet and François Matheron

Translated and with a Preface by

Jeffrey Mehlman

COLUMBIA UNIVERSITY PRESS

New York

Columbia University Press wishes to express its appreciation
for assistance given by the government of France through
Le Ministère de la Culture in the preparation of this translation.

COLUMBIA UNIVERSITY PRESS
Publishers since 1893
New York   Chichester, West Sussex

Ecrits sur la psychanalyse:
Freud et Lacan, © Stock/IMEC, 1993. Translation ©
Columbia University Press, 1996
All rights reserved

Library of Congress Cataloguing-in-Publication Data
Althusser, Louis.
[Ecrits sur la psychanalyse, English]
Writings on psychoanalysis : Freud and Lacan / Louis Althusser;
edited by Olivier Corpet and François Matheron ; translated and with
a preface by Jeffrey Mehlman.
p.   cm. — (European Perspectives)
Includes bibliographical references and index.
ISBN 0-231-10169-4 (pbk.)
1. Freud, Sigmund, 1856–1939. 2. Lacan, Jacques, 1901–
3. Psychoanalysis. I. Corpet, Olivier. II. Matheron, François. III. Title.
BF109.F74A82513 1996
150.19'5—dc20   96–25626
CIP

Casebound editions of Columbia University Press books are
printed on permanent and durable acid-free paper.

Printed in the United States of America
Designed by Nicola Ferguson

c 10 9 8 7 6 5 4 3 2 1
p 10 9 8 7 6 5 4 3 2

Contents

———

Translator's Preface

Early in *The Future Lasts Forever,* Louis Althusser's memoir of a life of Marxist theory that came to a sudden halt with the strangling of his wife (in what was determined to be a bout of temporary insanity), the author shares with his readers a persistent adolescent fantasy: his wish to have the first name *Jacques.* He proceeds to read the name almost as a rebus: *J* would indicate a *jet* of sperm; the deep *a* would bind Louis (become "Jacques") to his father Charles; the terminal *ques* would become a phallic *queue* or tail; and the whole would hint at those peasant revolts known in French as *Jacqueries.* This volume, which assembles materials charting Althusser's intense and ambivalent relation with the thought and career of Jacques Lacan, might well be viewed as the germination of that seminal fantasy.

For Althusser's influential reading of Marx was in crucial respects an effort to interpret his thought in a manner congruent with Lacan's reading of Freud. Lacan's Freud was a virtuoso rendition of the (falsely) dualist myth of Narcissus in counterpoint with the triangular rhythms of Oedipus, as though the treble part in some turn-of-the-century *mitteleuropäische* suite had been written in 2/4 time and the bass in 3/4. Althusser, it now appears, tried something similar. The Lacanian narcissistic-imaginary became the Althusserian realm of ideology, a world of mirror reflections and edifying humanist myths, culminating in what Kundera would call the Grand March—in 2/4 time—of utopian revolution.

The Lacanian Oedipal, on the other hand, became the gateway to structure and/as the touchstone of (intellectual) maturity. Althusser would chide Lacan for his fidelity to Lévi-Strauss and would insist that *his* notion of structure, in its irreducible dispersion, was not Lévi-Straussian at all. When Deleuze and Guattari did their best to show that the ¾ *oompah-pah* of Lacan's Oedipal polka might be subject to ridicule, Althusser may have felt unthreatened. (Foucault, after all, had not yet opened the second—counter-Marxian—front in the anti-structuralist offensive.) But the fact that the crucial break between the "ideological" (humanist) youth of Marx and his structural(ist) maturity might be figured as an epistemological cut, or *coupure*, was unmistakable: more than an influence from Bachelard, who spoke of epistemological "obstacles," the notion of a crucial discontinuity or cut figuring the leap into structure was a borrowing and transformation of the "castration complex" of Lacan's Freud. Jac-*ques* indeed....

As for the "Jacquerie," the radical political import ascribed to Lacan's undertaking, here is Althusser in a letter to Lacan of 10 December 1963, during the heady first days of their alliance: "One can always escape the financial and social effects of a social revolution.... [But] I am speaking of a different revolution, the one you are preparing without [your adversaries] knowing it, one from which no sea in the world will ever be able to protect them, and no respectability, whether capitalist or socialist, the one that will deprive them of the security of their Imaginary...." The true revolution, beyond "socialist" respectability, was to be by way of analytic theory.

In retrospect, it appears that in its heyday the world of French theory was a matter of two opposing alliances. The first was that of Lacan and Althusser; the second may perhaps be dated from Deleuze's challenge to Foucault: "If I take on Freud, will you take care of Marx?"[1] This book is the rich record of the first of those alliances, and of its breakup. In the beginning we find Althusser acting out another of the principal fantasies he ascribed to himself in his memoirs: that of playing "father to one's father." For, on the one hand, we see him in the role of Lacan's disciple, a veritable John the Baptist ("I am prophesying: but we have entered, and in large measure thanks to you, into an era in which one can at last be a prophet in one's own country"), and, on the other, he is Lacan's protector and benefactor, arranging the administrative coup that brought Lacan to lecture in the Salle Dussane of the Ecole Normale Supérieure during the glory years of the late 1960s. We see Althusser playing spiritual director to his own analyst, René Diatkine, in two long letters. "Father to his father" again, he informs his analyst, a fervent anti-Lacanian, that without Lacan there is no "salvation."

The religious metaphor may provide our best guide to the breakdown of the alliance, for Althusser remained a man who basked in the bonds of organized solidarity: first the Catholic church, then the German stalag (where he was a prisoner of war for five years), and finally the French Communist party. All helped define the principal mode of happiness he was to know. If, however, there is a constant in Lacan's thought, it lies in the will to escape from precisely such forms of solidarity: the postwar essay on the prisoner's dilemma, the seminar on "The Purloined Letter," and the dissolution of the Ecole freudienne all provide evidence of that compulsion.

Shall we say that the extraordinarily influential and productive encounter between Lacan and Althusser was a mismatch? Perhaps. For Althusser's carping remarks about Lacan in his first paper for the Tbilisi colloquium on the unconscious almost suggest as much. In the end, the Lacanian will to heterogeneity found Althusser more interested in the frightened analysts trying to contain the heterodoxy of Lacan at the time he was dissolving *their* Ecole than in Lacan himself. Lacan, slated to be a new prophet for the age, had become less an inspiring or castigating father than an intimidating pre-Oedipal mother, as Althusser claimed in a manic performance before the panicking analysts of the Ecole freudienne in March 1980. For the alliance it was a final, vexed stand. Althusser would be overwhelmed by his personal tragedy a few months later. Lacan would die the following year. An intellectual era of extraordinary brilliance had come to an end.[2]

Notes

1. As for Derrida, readers of this volume will be surprised to find an argument of his (concerning letters that by no means always arrive at their destination) invoked by Althusser without attribution and used against Lacan when their alliance was foundering.

2. This volume does not include two texts published in the original French edition: a working paper on the typology of discourse types (scientific, ideological, aesthetic, unconscious), "Trois Notes sur la théorie des discours" (1966), and a brief piece challenging the primacy of transference over the countertransference in analytic theory, "Sur le transfert et le contre-transfert" (1973).

—*Jeffrey Mehlman*

Introduction

WRITINGS ON PSYCHOANALYSIS constitutes the first of three volumes of theoretical writings by Louis Althusser envisaged by Editions Stock and the Institut Mémoires de l'Edition Contemporaine. The idea for the anthology developed and grew as we explored Louis Althusser's archives. Far from being limited to a single article ("Freud and Lacan"), to a few episodes (the "Tbilisi affair" or the dissolving of the Ecole freudienne de Paris), and a personal experience, Louis Althusser's relation to psychoanalysis was also—emphatically—a theoretical one. It began rather early. In fact, if we can believe his personal diary, Althusser delivered a talk on child analysis on November 13, 1959, which was probably continued on November 16, but no trace of it remains in his archives. On November 16 or 19, Emmanuel Terray, one of his students at the time, spoke on the "psychoanalysis of psychoses"; plainly intrigued by the lecture, which was centered on Freud but also evoked Melanie Klein, Althusser retained his notes. On December 3, 1959, Alain Badiou spoke about Lacan, and Althusser's appointment book contains the following note for December 11: "introduction to Lacan." First stirrings.

When Louis Althusser, during the academic year 1963–1964, offered a seminar on psychoanalysis, and more specifically on Lacan, it was thus not the first time he spoke—or had others speak—on the subject at the Ecole Normale Supérieure. The 1959 talks do not appear to have been pursued as part of any collective effort, but such was not the case for those of 1963–1964. At the time Althusser had already organized two seminars to which the students of the Ecole Normale Supérieure had made significant contributions, one in 1961–1962 on the young Marx and another in 1962–1963 on the origins of structuralism, with Althusser himself discussing "Foucault and the problematic of origins" and then "Lévi-Strauss in search of his alleged forebears." This time the aim was more ambitious: what was plainly at stake for Althusser was constituting a collective effort commensurate with the theoretical demands of the day.

When he undertook to organize his seminar on psychoanalysis,[1] Louis Althusser assigned a reading of Lacan to students barely familiar with him. Conjointly he orchestrated the arrival of Lacan at the Ecole Normale Supérieure, with Lacan's inaugural presentation taking place there on January 15, 1964. From the time of its installation in that prestigious institution, Lacanian psychoanalysis was regarded as one of the principal poles of the French intellectual scene.[2]

Louis Althusser may never have planned to publish a work solely devoted to psychoanalysis, but the bulk and richness of the available texts, the continuity that in a sense links them but also the discontinuities, the breaks, and occasionally the slippages and regressions, all bear the mark of an intellectual adventure sufficiently autonomous to merit separate publication. Since such a volume would be significantly stripped of meaning without the article "Freud and Lacan," we have taken the risk of undoing what Althusser undertook, for it will be recalled that this text, published in a journal in 1964, was reprinted in a collection, *Positions*, that appeared in 1976. Unlike *For Marx*, that volume was less a homogeneous book than an assemblage of articles intended, at a specific conjuncture, to supply the traces and construct the image of an itinerary whose unity remains problematic.

The writings published in this volume are not the only texts of Louis Althusser related to psychoanalysis, a domain that left a profound imprint on his existence. After a first analysis begun in 1950 and interrupted in the fall of 1963, Louis Althusser took on René Diatkine, definitively, as his analyst; Diatkine's name appears for the first time in his appointment book on October 30, 1964. Numerous traces of that ongoing endeavor have been rediscovered in his archives, in particular dream narratives and fragments of a "journal" in large part concerned with the progress of his own analysis. Although it is quite clear that such documents are not foreign to his theoretical activity, their status is nonetheless quite separate; our first concern has thus been to clearly distinguish such "analytic material" from the theoretical writings, which are the only ones published in this collection. Our aim has been to confront the reader with as exhaustive an assemblage of texts as possible, in full awareness of the possibility of subsequent discoveries outside the personal archives kept by Louis Althusser. Some of these texts were published by Louis Althusser himself: "Freud and Lacan" and "On Marx and Freud"; another was published without his consent: "The Discovery of Dr. Freud." The "Letters to D." may not have been intended for publication, but Louis Althusser circulated them, as he did "Three Notes on the Theory of Discourses," an extremely ambitious working document. We do not know what fate was intended for "On Transference and Countertransference," for Althusser rewrote it from a first version titled "Small Portable Incongruities."* We may assume, however, that he did so with an "idea in mind." Finally, it appears that he composed his "Open Letter to Analysands and Analysts in Solidarity with Jacques Lacan" with the thought—which was deliberately or inadvertently abandoned rather hastily—that he was going to be able to publish it.

We are publishing at the end of this volume the entirety of the correspondence we have been able to find between Louis Althusser and Jacques Lacan. An exceptional document, this collection of letters casts valuable light on one of the constants of the texts presented to the reader in this volume: the massive and ambivalent presence of the work and person of Jacques Lacan. Lacan, who is present even to the point of Althusser's choice of an admittedly non–Lacanian analyst, but one who had himself been in analysis with Lacan and to whom Althusser sent two theoretical letters devoted to Lacan. Lacan, concerning whom Althusser's library, refuting once again the often flaunted ignorance of *The Future Lasts Forever*, reveals to us that Althusser had read and annotated most of his texts long before the publication of *Ecrits* in 1966. Lacan, concerning whom Althusser wrote to his friend Franca,[3]

> One of my predictions has come true. I had foretold that Lacan would ask to see me. The summit meeting took place this evening, and I am just returning from it. Quite moving. A man broken by his enemies, shattered, yet still replete with genius, but doubting his era and all that he might expect of it. I told him that things would change, that all he need accord me is a year and he would already see the results. Plainly, he is attracted, but he has little faith in it all. His error in allowing himself to live enclosed in as artificial a world as possible, that of medicine.

Lacan, whom Althusser will have come to the Ecole Normale Supérieure when the psychoanalyst leaves Sainte-Anne and of whom he will write to Franca on January 21, 1964, a week after the inaugural session: "Lacan gave his first 'seminar' after the drama of his break with a portion of his former students at the Ecole last Wednesday. The entirety of a long section of my letter (the first long letter, the only one I sent him, the one where there are fish—not the one on Nietzsche ...)[4] entered into his reflection," before adding on the subject of the seminar, "I don't attend, which is the height of bliss. Absence. A strange absence. There are strange absences, good absences." Lacan, the texts of whose seminars (which he would not attend) Althusser would read shortly thereafter, seminars that sickness would in any event have prevented him from hearing. Lacan, of whom he would speak once again to Franca in a letter of October 25, 1964: "Have read the typed transcript of the lectures delivered by Lacan here while I was in the house at Epinay. Didn't understand everything, far from it, but finally something from time to time ... I read pencil in hand, annotating, annotating annotating." But Lacan, against whom Althusser's thought on the notion of the subject would come and who is quite present in "Three Notes on the Theory of Discourses." Lacan, of whom Althusser would write in a letter to Lucien Sève on March 28, 1973, that "one of the rare points one owes to him" is having distinguished psychoanalysis from psychology, having shown that "psychoanalysis is concerned with unconscious fantasies and their effects." Lacan, run into one last time in March 1980.

It would be risky to attempt a final assessment of what had no ambition of being a finished work. No one would say so better than Louis Althusser himself, who, renowned for his theoretical rectifications, knew as well on occasion how to indulge in what is perhaps a more perilous exercise: the adducing of the sheer limits of his undertakings, which he realized were the inevitable counterpart of his untimely questions. Asked about the relations between the unconscious and ideology, the problem at the heart of his reflections on psychoanalysis, Althusser replies as follows to a friend, in an undated letter, which was probably written in 1977:

> The only thing that I can tell you with some certainty (given that I entertain very distant relations with what I may have written) is that I stopped short (quite clearly) before the question that interests you about the "relations" between ideology (or concrete ideological formations) and the unconscious. I have said that there must be some re-

lation there, but at the same time I forbade myself from inventing it—considering that it was for me a problem provisionally without solution, for myself or perhaps not only for myself—for myself in any event. And naturally in refusing to go any further, I refused to follow those well-known figures who had attempted to go further, such as Reich or others. The place where I went the furthest must be in the final notes for the article "Freud and Lacan," but there too, in the articles on state ideological apparatuses, there is a limit that has not been crossed. Thus, when you level at me "the question" "How do you see a conceptual elaboration between the unconscious and ideology?" I can only reply that I don't see it. If Freud were alive (and thought today what he thought during his lifetime) and you were able to ask him, "How do you see the elaboration of the relation between biology and the unconscious?" he would more or less tell you what he wrote, namely, that there is surely a relation, but that he did not see how to elaborate it conceptually. Every question does not necessarily imply an answer.

Whereas Louis Althusser's correspondence reveals the speed with which he wrote, certain texts having been composed in a few days, his archives also show us the care with which he revised his writings, cut or added passages, and implemented corrections that were not always matters of mere detail. Without succumbing to the dizzying delights of philological or genetic criticism, we have assumed the task of publishing as notes those variants that, rightly or wrongly, seemed to us to bear significantly on his work.** In addition, in our introductions we have drawn on the complete set of documents to which we had access, and in particular on Althusser's extraordinary correspondence with Franca. We do not claim to present *the* truth about these texts, but we are convinced that the epistolary excerpts in this volume will teach those willing to read them something about the writings of Louis Althusser, and not simply about their author. To those surprised to find a private correspondence massively invoked in the introduction to a theoretical effort, we merely counter with what Jean-Pierre Lefebvre has already written in his new translation of Hegel's *Phenomenology of Mind*: "To those bothered by the substance of this introduction to the subject, the translator might simply say that all these reminders serve to designate the era from which he would propose a return to the text by way of a new translation: an era in which—and not, moreover, without difficulty—the consecrated discourse of major works is subordinated to questions of time, including the most repressed of questions, although it is at the heart of one of the chapters of the *Phenomenology*, that of the relation between men and women, and of the cultural attributes of each. In 1807, in 1991."[5] To which we would simply add: in 1993.

Louis Althusser's writings have been ordered chronologically, with the special status of the correspondence with Jacques Lacan dictating its presence at the end of the volume. Each text or group of texts is preceded by an introduction based on the complete set of documents available in the Althusser archives, whose fruitfulness, once again, proves to be exceptional.

Out of concern for both faithfulness to the documents in question and readability of the texts, we have corrected slips of the pen or errors and omissions of punctuation, occasionally adding in brackets the words indispensable for understanding a sentence or restoring proper syntax, and have supplied in the notes the needed biobibliographical references or indications of fact. All underlinings in manuscript or typed texts appear as italics. Finally, unless otherwise indicated (and specifically in the text "Freud and Lacan"), all notes are those of the editors.

We would like to thank all those who have helped us in the preparation of this volume, and above all François Boddaert, Louis Althusser's heir, who has not been sparing in the trust he has shown us. Our thanks are extended to Yann Moulier-Boutang, whose biographical efforts devoted to Althusser and the precious documents he located and identified for us have been extremely important, but also to Elisabeth Roudinesco, whose knowledge of the history of psychoanalysis and whose intellectual generosity have been a consistent and irreplaceable resource. To Etienne Balibar and the documents he has generously entrusted to the Institut Mémoires de l'Edition Contemporaine (IMEC) we owe the opportunity to have contributed several indispensable rectifications concerning some of those texts. We also thank Jacques-Alain Miller, who has authorized and encouraged us to publish the letters of Jacques Lacan, as well as René Diatkine, Jacques Nassif, Peter Schöttler, and Michel Tort, who have furnished us with extremely useful documents and information, and finally, all our collaborators at IMEC, particularly Sandrine Samson, whose support has been indispensable.

Olivier Corpet
François Matheron

1

Freud and Lacan

1964

WHEN LOUIS ALTHUSSER *published his article "Freud and Lacan" in* La Nouvelle Critique *(Dec. 1964–Jan. 1965), no. 161–62, the official journal of Communist intellectuals, it was hardly his first effort in that direction. He had already spoken of Lacan in the article "Philosophy and Human Sciences," which appeared in the* Revue de l'enseignement philosophique *(June–July 1963), and specifically in a note republished in "Freud and Lacan." As early as 1960 he had wanted to produce the effect of a proper name in his text "On the Young Marx," published in* La Pensée *(Mar.–Apr. 1961) and included in* For Marx. *After the word* scan *in the sentence "It is the necessity of their life that we scan through our understanding of their nodes, their references, and their shifts,"[1] he had initially envisaged the following note, which he ultimately abandoned: "I borrow this term from Jacques Lacan. Among those dis-*

ciplines attentive to events and major advents, there are no doubt correspondences and affinities that a single word is capable of freeing from the rest."

The major part of *"Freud and Lacan"* was written at the end of January and the beginning of February 1964, at a time when Althusser's intellectual and political activity was particularly intense. The publication in August 1963 of *"On the Materialist Dialectic"* in La Pensée no. 110 provoked a violent response from certain leaders of the French Communist Party, particularly Roger Garaudy and Gilbert Mury; several meetings were held at party headquarters. In the course of one of them, which he experienced as though it were a political trial, Althusser read on November 30, 1963, an extremely violent answer to his critics[2] that he later sent for publication to Marcel Cornu, managing editor of La Pensée, along with his article *"Marxism and Humanism,"* which had been written in October. On November 10, 1963, he wrote his friend Franca, "I am going to write a first book of Marxist theory, a book of very general themes. Then I will write a book of historical studies on Marx, Lenin, and so on," and he announced to her on January 23, 1964, "I have written 80 pages of the book in two days." Unfortunately no trace of them has been found. On January 31 he wrote to her of the forthcoming publication of an issue of La Pensée "entirely done by us (my students and myself) on technocracy and humanism." Although that collection would never see the day, Althusser nonetheless did write a text titled *"Technocracy and Humanism,"* which was rediscovered in his archives. On December 6, 1963, he delivered an extended introductory presentation at the seminar of Pierre Bourdieu and Jean-Claude Passeron, which was recorded and preserved. In the field of psychoanalysis per se, the article *"Freud and Lacan"* was directly linked to the seminar on psychoanalysis organized by Althusser at the Ecole Normale Supérieure as of November 1963 and to the relations established with Lacan, whose seminar he would welcome to the Ecole in January 1964.[3] This period of frenetic activity would culminate in a period of serious depression and hospitalization.

The submerged but (at least retrospectively) perceptible violence of *"Freud and Lacan"* owes a good deal to the context in which it was written. To the elements just noted should be added a more "intimate" dimension. At the beginning of September 1963 Althusser learned of the suicide of his friend Jacques Martin,[4] a terrifying event for him that was still very much present at the beginning of 1964. Reviewing for Franca on February 15 the recent accumulation of painful—and occasionally comical—situations surrounding him, he came to evoke his text: "And in several of these situations hidden by the great silence you are aware of, the death of J[acques] M[artin]. Something of that whole situation, about which I decided not to tell you at B., has made its way into a few sentences or a few words of my article on Lacan. I spoke to you about it through him. An article written with a little life, a little blood, and a good deal of death." And the finest commentary, a surprising moment for readers of Reading "Capital," on the hallucinatory state in which Althusser's writing was produced, was given by Althusser himself in another letter to Franca, of February 21, 1964:

> Everything always transpires like this: as if, beyond all I told you in my last letter about my "charges" and their resolution, there had also been that extraordinary sort of direct experience, of almost unmediated contact with certain realities that are normally unbearable—I mean unbearable in the daily contact that people have with life: stories of life and death, of which something had filtered into that text on Lacan I left you. A rather strange thing, when I think of it. I have truly lived several months with an extraordinary capacity for bare contact with some profound realities, feeling them, seeing them, reading them in individuals and in reality as in an open book. Have often thought about that extraordinary thing while thinking about the situation of the rare individuals whose names I venerate, Spinoza, Marx, Nietzsche, Freud, and who must necessarily have had that contact to be able to write what they left; otherwise, I don't see how they could have lifted that enormous deposit, that gravestone covering over the real . . . so as to have that direct contact which still burns in them for all eternity.

Although the article "Freud and Lacan" was published in La Nouvelle Critique, *a politically crucial site for a Communist intellectual, that was not its original destination. Althusser had first envisaged its publication in the small* Revue de l'enseignement philosophique, *where he had already published several articles. Apparently fatigued by the absence of any clear reply from that journal, Althusser sent his text on August 23, 1964, to his friend Marcel Cornu. The project then changed character: he was now dealing with a journal,* La Pensée, *that, although not an official organ of the Communist Party, was directly linked to it. And although the violent hostility of the immediate postwar period had subsided, psychoanalysis continued to be the object of great mistrust and, above all, of vertiginous ignorance within the party. Even though Marcel Cornu, who always supported Althusser, was quite favorable to publication, he was not necessarily master of his acts. When Althusser wrote him, in his accompanying letter, "This text is, in its way, a bombshell, but one that runs no risk of releasing into the air any explosions capable of wounding us—neither you nor me. People will bitch, but since they don't know what I'm talking about, they will have to study the problem before they risk contradicting me," Marcel Cornu, a man of political awareness, immediately answered him in an undated letter that if the silence of Communist publications on the subject of psychoanalysis absolutely must be broken, his text "will seem, in fact, after the long silence, like a damned atomic bomb." Cornu consequently asked him to add a few sentences offering political assurances. Although that request was to all appearances minor, it did not augur well. Althusser thus wrote to Franca on September 30, 1964, "Must tell you as well that I have just added a long preliminary note and several short notes to my paper on Freud and Lacan, and that I hope that they will agree to publish it in this form. . . . Interdictions weigh long on the damned, even when death has shut their mouth," and in an undated letter, he specifies to her, "I have the worst problems concerning the publication of my paper on Lacan. At* La Pensée *they're trembling. What asses! I think I'll send it to the* Osservatore Romano.*" Althusser proceeded in vain: the article would not be published in* La Pensée. *He then sent it to* La Nouvelle Critique, *whose editor-in-chief was his friend Jacques Arnault and where he had just published his article "Student Problems" (no. 152 in Jan. 1964). In a period of utter turmoil, the journal accepted the text. And thus it was, through a curious wink of history, that the article "Freud and Lacan" appeared in the journal in which a resounding condemnation of "psychoanalysis, a reactionary ideology," had been published in 1949.*[5]

It is always precarious to assess the posterity of a text, and even more of an article. Frequently quoted but republished only in 1976 in Positions,[6] *it was no doubt barely read by subsequent generations, even if it had circulated in the early 1970s in a pirate edition published by "Editions des grandes têtes molles de notre époque." It did not give rise to any genuine dialogue with Lacan. Even if Lacan congratulated Althusser warmly when he received a typed version, his letter of July 6, 1964, published in this collection, is at bottom rather politely formal. Although Althusser would continue to be interested in Lacan's work until the end, the obverse was not the case. We will cite in conclusion Althusser's remarks on him in a letter to Franca of September 17, 1966:*

> *Reread several pages of Lacan after having written my text on psychoanalysis.*[7] *This is always how these things happen; it's quite disarming: now I understand him!! for the good reason that (1) he says what I say when he says good things (but go figure out whether, without realizing it and even because I hadn't understood him, it's not I myself who am rehashing what he says!![)] (there must be phenomena of understanding that are quite unconscious); (2) I see precisely the point where he gets "unhinged"; (3) and in addition I see that I hadn't understood him when I wrote that article on him (I had understood his importance, but not what he meant). What is all the same rather vexing is that, given our relations, when I wrote that paper on him, he could have told me: "This is good, full of good will, but you haven't understood what I meant; I'll*

explain it to you." No. Silence. It is true that knowing that someone has not understood *something is tantamount to seizing and possessing and* retaining *a great advantage over him, and that this advantage can be kept only by* maintaining silence about *it. It's "human," as they say. I can see quite well the logic of that attitude, sensing at times the same sort of satisfaction in myself: seeing someone say nonsense and being in a position to correct him; the temptation to keep one's peace is quite great and provides a number of advantages. One is aware that one "has" the fool at one's disposition, but one reserves one's advantage, and all the while one has the spectacle of a guy who* believes *he has understood. It's enough to let him continue; he can only do himself in, which doubles the advantage one has over him. In the last analysis, this is valid for adversaries, but for friends . . . I have trained my young friends in a different method, and I rejoice in it. I must not be "orthodox"; however, without that "other method," there is no* collective *effort possible. Perhaps that is all we have done—shown, in any event, that collective work in philosophy was possible and oh how profitable! (perhaps for the first time; I'm not speaking of "master-disciple" relations, which are classic, but of relations of equality in one's exchanges, for that is what collective work is).*

There is thus an Althusserian method of collective work, as may be seen in the case of "Three Notes on the Theory of Discourses."

The Althusser archives contain two distinct typed versions of the article "Freud and Lacan," which was thus typed at least twice at the same typewriter, each version containing numerous handwritten corrections. We publish here the version of the text chosen by Althusser, while indicating the variants that have seemed particularly significant, particularly the passage on Sartre originally envisaged for the conclusion of the article, which Althusser commented on in these terms in a letter to Franca dated simply "Sunday night" and probably written at the beginning of February 1964:

Sending you a paper, another interrupted discourse on Lacan, Freud: the sole discourse that, as theoretical discourse, is the first to know itself without interruption. Read the last lines on Sartre; they are deliberate; he has to be forced out of his happy psychosis, and for that there is only the whip: strike him in the face with his own rods: words *(he's just published a book under that title, where he speaks of his childhood and says, 'I didn't have an Oedipus complex or almost not, and I have no superego"; when one considers that this sort of theoretical confusion—on other scores his right to be confused is sacred, like every human right to be what one is—takes the place of thought—or dispenses with thought—for who knows how many men, men who tell themselves that someone is thinking for them, is being free and daring for them, etc., vicarious daring and freedom—*

and even then, if it were genuine daring or freedom! but this delirium!! I see a whip to the face as the only means of imposing silence on such imposture, restoring it in the process to either silence or literature—or therapy).

Then he adds enigmatically, "the last lines as a warning (to Sartre), but the rest is good, and I subscribe to it."

We are publishing, as an appendix, the "editor's note" accompanying Ben Brewster's original English translation of "Freud and Lacan," which first appeared in 1969 in New Left Review *and then was incorporated in the collection* Lenin and Philosophy and Other Essays *(London:* NLB, *1971).*

Freud and Lacan

Preliminary Note

Let us say so directly: whoever today wants quite simply to understand Freud's revolutionary discovery, not merely to recognize its existence, but also to know its meaning, must traverse, at the cost of huge critical and theoretical efforts, the immense span of ideological prejudices that separate us from Freud. For not only was Freud's discovery, as will be seen, reduced to disciplines that are, in essence, foreign to it (biology, psychology, sociology, philosophy); not only have numerous psychoanalysts (notably of the American school) become accomplices of that revisionism; but in addition, that revisionism has itself objectively served the prodigious ideological exploitation whose target and victim psychoanalysis has been. It is not without reason that formerly (in 1948) French Marxists denounced in that exploitation a "reactionary ideology" serving in the ideological struggle against Marxism and as a practical means of intimidation and mystification.

But it can be said today that those same Marxists were, in their way, directly or indirectly, the first victims of the ideology they were denouncing, since they confused it with Freud's revolutionary discovery, thus accepting the positions of the adversary, submitting to his own conditions, and acknowledging in the image he foisted on them the alleged reality of psychoanalysis. The entire history of the relations between Marxism and psychoanalysis rests, in essence, on that confusion and that imposture.

That it was particularly difficult to escape that past may first of all be understood in terms of that ideology's function, the "dominant" ideas having, in this case, performed to perfection their role of "domination," imposing themselves unwittingly on the very minds intent on combating them. But it may also be understood in terms of the existence of the psychoanalytic revisionism that made that exploitation possible: the fall into ideology in effect began with the fall of psychoanalysis into biologism, psychologism, and sociologism.

This revisionism was able to achieve authority by virtue of the ambiguity of certain concepts from Freud, who, like every inventor, was constrained to think his discovery in terms of existing theoretical concepts, which were thus constituted for other ends. (Was not Marx also constrained to think through his discovery in certain Hegelian terms?) Nothing in this should surprise anyone who is at all apprised of the history of new sciences—and concerned to delineate what is irreducible in a discovery and its object within the concepts that expressed it at its birth and that, having become untimely through the progress of knowledge, may subsequently conceal it.

To return to Freud today thus requires

1. not only that one reject as a crude mystification the ideological layer of its reactionary exploitation

2. but that one avoid falling into the ambiguities—which are more subtle and sustained by the prestige of several more or less scientific disciplines—of psychoanalytic revisionism

3. and that one devote oneself, finally, to a serious labor of historical-theoretical criticism intent on identifying and defining, within the concepts Freud was obliged to employ, the true *epistemological relation* existing between those concepts and the content that he was thinking.

Without that triple labor of ideological critique (nos. 1 and 2) and epistemological elucidation (no. 3), which was practically inaugurated in France by Lacan, Freud's discovery, in its specificity, will remain outside our reach. What is more serious, moreover, is that we will accept as Freud precisely what has been placed in our reach, whether we want to refuse it (the reactionary ideological exploitation) or, more or less unreflectively, we subscribe to it (the different forms of bio-psycho-sociological revisionism). In both cases we would remain captive, at different levels, of the explicit or implicit categories of ideological exploitation and theoretical revisionism. Marxists, who know from experience what distortions Marx's adversaries imposed on his thought, can understand that Freud may have been subject in his way to the same fate and what the importance of an authentic "return to Freud" is.

They will be prepared to admit that an article as brief as this one, which proposes to broach a problem of this importance, if it is not to betray the problem, must restrict itself to the essential: situating the *object* of psychoanalysis, to give a first definition of it, in concepts allowing *localization*, an indispensable prerequisite for the elucidation of that object. They will also be prepared to admit as a consequence that concepts be made to intervene, insofar as is possible, in their rigorous form, as in any scientific discipline, without either diluting them in an all too approximate popularizing commentary or undertaking to develop them truly in an analysis that would demand an entirely different amount of space.

The serious study of Freud and Lacan, which anyone can undertake, will alone yield the exact measure of those concepts and will allow one to define the problems left hanging in a theoretical reflection already rich in results and promises.

L.A.

Friends have reproached me, quite rightly, with having spoken of Lacan in a few lines:[1] to have spoken about him too much for what I said on the subject and too little for what I concluded from it. They have asked me for a few words justifying my allusion and its object. Here they are—a few words, where a book would be needed.

In the history of Western reason, births are the object of all sorts of care, anticipation, precaution, preventive measures, and so on. Prenatal therapy is institutional. When a new science is born, the family circle is always already prepared for astonishment, jubilation, and baptism. For a long time now every child, even a foundling, is reputed to be the son of a father, and when he is a prodigy, fathers would be fighting each other off at the ticket window were it not for the mother and the respect owed her. In our replete world a space is anticipated for birth; a space is anticipated even for the anticipation of birth: "prospective."

To my knowledge, in the course of the nineteenth century, two or three children were born who were not expected: Marx, Nietzsche, Freud. They were "natural," or illegitimate, children, in the sense that nature offends customs, law, morality, and the consecrated skills of life: nature is the rule violated, the unwed mother, and thus the absence of a legal father. A child without a father is made to pay dearly by Western reason. Marx, Nietzsche, and Freud had to pay the (occasionally atrocious) bill of survival, a price calculable in exclusions, insults, misery, hunger, and deaths or madness. I speak only of them (one could speak of other accursed figures who experienced their death sentence in paint, sounds, or poetry). I speak only of them because they were the birth of sciences or of criticism.

That Freud knew poverty, slander, and persecution, that his soul was sufficiently well anchored to bear, while interpreting them, all the insults of the century, is perhaps not unrelated to some of the limits and impasses of his genius. Let us leave that point, whose examination is no doubt premature. Consider merely Freud's solitude and his time. I am not speaking of human solitude (he had teachers and friends, even though he knew poverty); I am speaking of his *theoretical* solitude. For when he decided to think, that is, to express in the form of a rigorous system of abstract concepts, the extraordinary discovery he reencountered every day in his *practice,* he searched in vain for theoretical precedents, fathers in theory; he found barely any. He was forced to submit to and make the best of the following theoretical situation: being his own father unto himself, constructing with his own artisan's hands the theoretical space in which to situate his discovery, weaving with borrowed threads, taken left and right, by guesswork, the great knotted web in which to catch, in the depths of blind experience, the redundant fish of the unconscious, which men call mute because it speaks even while they sleep.

This means, to express it in Kant's terms, that Freud had to think his discovery and his practice in imported concepts borrowed from the then dominant energy physics, political economy, and biology of his time. No legal heritage behind him, except for a mass of philosophical concepts (consciousness, preconscious, unconscious, etc.) perhaps more burdensome than fertile, since they were marked by a problem of consciousness present even in its restrictions; no fund left by any ancestor whatever, for his only predecessors were writers—Sophocles, Shakespeare, Molière, Goethe—aphorisms, and so on. Theoretically Freud set up shop on his own, producing his own concepts, his "domestic" concepts, beneath the cover of imported concepts borrowed from the state of existing sciences and, it must be said, within the horizon of the ideological world in which those concepts were immersed.

Thus it was that we received Freud. A long sequence of texts that were profound, at times clear, at times obscure, often enigmatic and contradictory, problematic, armed with concepts of which many at first sight seem no longer valid, inadequate to their object, outmoded.

For today we do not at all doubt the existence of that content: analytic practice itself, its effect.

Let me summarize, then, the object that Freud is for us:

1. a practice (analytic therapy),

2. a technique (the method of therapy), which leads to an abstract exposition of theoretical aspect, and

3. a theory that relates to the practice and the technique.

That organic set—practice (1), technique (2), and theory (3)—reminds us of the structure of every scientific discipline. *Formally* what Freud gives us does indeed possess the structure of a science. I say "formally" because the difficulties of Freud's conceptual terminology, the occasionally palpable disproportion between his concepts and their content, lead me to raise the following question: in that organic set of practice-technique-theory, are we dealing with a truly stabilized set, one truly fixed at the scientific level? In other words, is the theory in this case truly a theory in the scientific sense? Is it not, on the contrary, a simple methodological transposition of the practice (therapy)? Whence the quite commonly accepted idea that beneath its scientific exterior (due to a respectable, but vain, ambition in Freud himself), psychoanalysis would remain a simple practice occasionally yielding results, but not always; a simple practice prolonged as a technique (the rules of the analytic method) but *without a theory*, at least without a true theory, what it declares as theory being no more than the blind technical concepts in which it thinks the rules of its practice; a simple practice without theory ... perhaps, then, quite simply *magic* (?) that would succeed as does every form of magic, through the effects of its prestige and its various forms of prestige, pressed into the service of a social need or demand, its sole reason, its true reason. Lévi-Strauss would have forged the theory of that *magic*, of the *social* practice that psychoanalysis would be, by designating the *shaman* as Freud's ancestor.

A practice pregnant with a partially silent theory? A practice proud or ashamed of being no more than the social magic of modern times? What then is psychoanalysis?

I

Lacan's first word is in order to say that, in principle, Freud founded a *science*, a new science that is the science of a new object: the unconscious.

This is a rigorous declaration. If psychoanalysis is indeed a science, since it is the science of its specific object, it is also a science according to the structure of every science, possessing a *theory* and a *technique* (method) that permit the knowledge and transformation of its object in a specific *practice*. As in any authentic constituted science, the practice is not the absolute of the science but a theoretically subordinated moment, the moment at which the theory become method (technique) enters into theoretical contact (knowledge) or practical contact (therapy) with its own object (the unconscious).

If that thesis is precise, analytic practice (therapy), which absorbs all the attention of interpreters and philosophers eager for the intimacy of the confidential couple and in which the confessions of the ill and professional medical secrecy exchange sacred vows of intersubjectivity, does not hold the secrets of psychoanalysis; it holds only a part of its reality, the one that exists in practice. It does not hold its theoretical secrets. If that thesis is precise, neither does the technique, a method, hold the secrets of psychoanalysis, unless it be, as with any method (i.e., by delegation), not of the practice but of the theory. Theory alone holds them, as in every scientific discipline.

In a hundred places in his work Freud said that he was a theorist; he compared psychoanalysis, with regard to scientificity, to the physical science emerging from Galileo and repeated that the practice (therapy) and analytic technique (the analytic method) were authentic only because they were based on a scientific *theory*. Freud said and repeated that a practice and a technique, even if fertile, would deserve the name "scientific" only if a theory granted them, not by simple declaration, but by rigorous foundation, the right to it.

Lacan's first word is to take that word literally and to draw the consequences, returning to Freud to seek out, discern, and delineate in him the theory from which all the rest emerged, the technique as much as the practice.

To return to Freud. Why this new return to sources? Lacan does not return to Freud like Husserl to Galileo or Thales, to grasp a birth at its birth—that is, to realize the religious philosophical prejudice regarding purity, which, like all water spurting into the light, is pure only at the very instant, at the pure instant, of its birth, at the pure passage from nonscience to science. For him, that passage is not pure but still impure. Purity comes after that passage; it is not in that residually "muddy" passage (the invisible mud of its past, suspended in the emergent water that feigns transparency—that is, innocence). To return to Freud means a return to the theory that is well established, well fixed, and well stabilized in Freud himself, to the mature, pondered, supported, verified theory, to the theory that is sufficiently advanced and settled within life (including practical life) to have built its home there, produced its method, and engendered its practice. The return to Freud is not a return to the birth of Freud but a return to his *maturity.* Freud's youth, the moving passage from not-yet-science to science (the period of his relations with Charcot, Bernheim, Breuer, until the *Studies on Hysteria* [1895]) may interest us, to be sure, but for an entirely different reason, either as an example of the archaeology of a science or as the negative index of nonmaturity, in which case we use it to date with certainty the maturity and its advent. The youth of a science is its maturity; before that age it is old, having the age of the prejudices on which it lives, like a child having the prejudices, and thus the age, of its parents.

That a young and thus mature theory can fall back into childhood, that is, into the prejudices of its elders and their descendants, is something that the entire history of psychoanalysis proves. That is the profound meaning of the return to Freud that Lacan proclaimed. We have to return to Freud to return to the maturity of Freudian theory, not to its childhood, but to its mature age, which is its true youth—we have to come back to Freud beyond the theoretical infantilism, the lapse back into childhood, in which a whole (and above all American) sector of contemporary psychoanalysis delights in the advantages of its surrenders.

This lapse back into childhood bears a name that phenomenologists will immediately understand: psychologism; alternatively, it bears another name that Marxists will immediately understand: pragmatism. The modern history of psychoanalysis illustrates Lacan's judgment. Western reason (juridical, religious, moral, and political *as well as* scientific reason) in fact consented, after years of misprision, scorn, and insults—means, moreover, that are always available should the occasion demand it—to conclude a pact of peaceful coexistence with psychoanalysis only on the condition of annexing it to its own sciences or its own myths: to psychology, be it behaviorist (Dalbiez), phenomenological (Merleau-Ponty), or existentialist (Sartre); to a more or less Jacksonian neurobiology (Ey); to "sociology" of a "culturalist" or "anthropological" stripe (dominant in the United States: Kardiner, M. Mead, etc.); and to philosophy—compare the "existential psychoanalysis" of Sartre, the *"Daseinanalyse"* of Binswanger, and so on. Psychoanalysts subscribed to those confusions, to that mythification of psychoanalysis, a discipline officially recognized at the cost of alliances and compromises sealed with *imaginary* lines of adoption but among very real powers, all too happy to emerge at last from their theoretical ghetto, to be "recognized" as full-fledged members of the great family of psychology, neurology, psychiatry, medicine, sociology, anthropology, philosophy, all too happy to affix to their practical success the label of the "theoretical" recognition that at last conferred on them, after decades of insults and exile, a right to exist in the world: that of science, medicine, and philosophy. They had not been wary of the agreement's suspicious cast, believing that the world was surrendering to their reason when in fact they themselves were surrendering, beneath the honors, to the reasons of that world, preferring its honors to its insults.

In so doing they were forgetting that a science is one only if it can fully pretend to dispose of its *own* specific object—which is its and its alone—and not of the congruent portion of an object borrowed, conceded, or abandoned by another science, of one of its "aspects," of its *residues*, which can always be accommodated in a variety of dishes in its own way, once the boss has been sated. In point of fact, if all psychoanalysis can be reduced to the "behaviorist" or Pavlovian "conditioning" of early childhood; if it can be reduced to a dialectic of the stages that Freud described under the terms *oral*, *anal*, and *genital* and the terms *latency* and *puberty*; if it can ultimately be reduced to the primal experience of the Hegelian struggle, the phenomenological *for the other*, or the "abyss" of Heideggerian being; if all psychoanalysis is no more than that art of accommodating the residues of neurology, biology, psychology, anthropology, and philosophy, what then remains to it as the specificity of its object, truly distinguishing it from those disciplines and making it a full-fledged science?[2]

It is at this point that Lacan intervenes to defend, against these "reductions" and deviations currently dominating a large portion of the theoretical interpretations of analysis, its irreducibility, which is but the *irreducibility of its object*. That this defense requires an uncommon lucidity and firmness, able to repel all the assaults of devouring hospitality by the aforementioned disciplines, is something that will be doubted by no one who even once measures the need for (theoretical, moral, social, economic) security, that is, the disquiet of guilds (whose status is indissolubly scientific-professional-juridical-economic) threatened in their equilibrium and comfort by the appearance of a singular discipline that forces every individual to inquire of himself not only about his discipline but about his reasons for believing in it, that is, for doubting it; by the appearance of a science that, to the extent that one believes in it, risks broaching existing boundaries and thus of modifying the status quo of several disciplines. Whence the contained passion, the impassioned contention of Lacan's language, which can live and survive only in a state of alert and prepossession: the language of a man already besieged and condemned by the crushing strength of threatened structures and guilds to anticipate their blows, at least to feign returning them before they have been received, thus discouraging the adversary from crushing him under its own. Whence also the often paradoxical recourse to the support of philosophies entirely alien to his scientific undertaking (Hegel, Heidegger), as if to so many intimidating witnesses, thrown in the face of some in order to exact their respect, as if to so many witnesses of a possible objectivity, the natural ally of his thought, to reassure or teach the others. This recourse has been quasi-indispensable in sustaining a discourse addressed *from within* solely to physicians, and one would have to be equally ignorant both of the conceptual feebleness of medical studies in general and of the best physicians' profound need for theory to condemn it without appeal. And since I am on the subject of his language, which for some accounts for all Lacan's prestige (the "Gongora of psychoanalysis," "Grand Dragon," great officiator of an esoteric cult in which gesture, silence, and compunction can together compose the ritual of genuine communication—as well as of a very "Parisian" fascination) and for others (scientists or philosophers of the first rank) accounts for his "artifice," his strangeness, and his "esoterism," one can see that it is not unrelated to the conditions of the exercise of his pedagogy: having to teach the theory of the unconscious to doctors, analysts, or analysands, Lacan gives them, in the rhetoric of his speech, the mimed equivalent of the language of the unconscious, which, as all know, is in its ultimate essence "*Witz*," pun, or metaphor, whether failed or successful, the equivalent of what they experience in their practice as either an analyst or a patient.

It is enough to understand the ideological and pedagogical conditions of that language—that is, to take the distance of historical and theoretical "exteriority" in relation to its pedagogical "interiority"—

to discern its objective meaning and import and to recognize its fundamental purpose: to give Freud's discovery theoretical concepts worthy of it by defining as rigorously as possible, today, *the unconscious* and its "laws," which constitute its entire object.

II

What is the *object* of psychoanalysis? It is that *with which* analytic technique has to deal in the analytic practice of therapy, that is, not the therapy itself, not that allegedly dual situation in which the first phenomenology or morality to come along can find the wherewithal to satisfy its need, but the "effects," prolonged in the surviving adult, of the extraordinary adventure that, from birth to the liquidation of the Oedipus complex, transforms a small animal engendered by a man and a woman into a little human child.

One of the "effects" of the becoming-human of the little biological being issuing from human childbirth is that there, in its place, is the object of psychoanalysis that bears the simple name of the *unconscious*.

That this little biological being survives, and instead of surviving as a child of the woods become the charge of wolves or bears (there *were* some of these, who were displayed in the princely courts of the eighteenth century) survives as a *human child* (having escaped all the deaths of childhood, of which many are human deaths, deaths sanctioning a failure of humanization), is the ordeal that all men, as adults, have surmounted: they are, *forever amnesiac,* the witnesses and quite often the victims of that victory, bearing in the deafest—that is, at the most vocal—recess of themselves the wounds, infirmities, and aches of that fight for human life or death. Some, most, emerge more or less unscathed—or at least make a point, out loud, of making it known; many of those former combatants remain marked by the experience for life; certain among them will die from their combat a bit later, old wounds suddenly reopened in a psychotic explosion, in madness, in the ultimate compulsion of a "negative therapeutic reaction"; others, who are more numerous, will die as "normally" as could be, under a cloak of "organic" failure. Humanity inscribes only its official deaths on its war memorials, those who managed to die on time, that is, late, men in human wars, in which only *human* wolves and gods sacrifice and tear each other apart. Psychoanalysis, in its sole survivors, is concerned with a different struggle, in the sole war without memoirs or memorials, which humanity pretends never to have fought, the one it thinks it has always won in advance, quite simply because its very existence is a function of having survived it, of living and giving birth to itself as culture within human culture. This is a war that, at every instant, is waged in each of its offspring, who, projected, deformed, rejected, each for himself, in solitude and against death, have to undertake the long forced march that turns mammalian larvae into human children, that is, *subjects*.

That the biologist will not find his affair in that object is certain; this business is not biological, since it is completely dominated, from the outset, by the obligatory constraint of the human order that every mother, beneath her maternal "love" or hatred, starting with the rhythm of feeding and training, engraves in the little sexed human animal. That history, "sociology," and anthropology will not find their affair in it is not at all astonishing, since they deal with society and thus with culture, that is, with what is no longer the little animal, who becomes human only for having traversed that infinite space that separates life from humanity, the biological from the historical, "nature" from "culture." That psychology should lose itself in that object is not at all strange, since it believes that it is dealing, in its "object," with some *human* "nature" or "nonnature," with the genesis of the being identified and registered under the very auspices of culture (of the human), whereas the object of psychoanalysis is the absolute a priori question, whether to be born or not to be [*le naître ou n'être pas*], the aleatory abyss of the human itself in every child of man. Of course "philosophy" loses its bearings [*repères*] and its haunts [*repaires*], since those singular origins would deprive it of the sole origins to which it pays homage in its being: God, reason, consciousness, history, and culture. It will be suspected that the object of psychoanalysis may be specific and that the modality of its matter and the specificity of its "mechanisms" (to use a word of Freud's) are of an entirely different order from the matter and the "mechanisms" that the biologist, the neurologist, the anthropologist, the sociologist, the psychologist, and the philosopher are impelled to know. It is enough to recognize that specificity, and thus the distinctness of the object underlying it, to recognize the radical right psychoanalysis has to the specificity of its concepts congruent with the specificity of its object: the unconscious and its effects.

III

Lacan would not dispute that without the emergence of a new science, *linguistics,* his own attempt at theorization would have been impossible. So goes the history of sciences, in which a science often becomes one only through the recourse to and diversion of other sciences, not only sciences existing at the time of its baptism, but also some new science, a latecomer needing time to be born. The provisional opaqueness of the shadow that the energy physics model of Helmholtz and Maxwell casts over Freudian theory has been dispersed today by the light that structural linguistics casts on its object, permitting a beginning of comprehension of that object. Freud had already said that everything was dependent on language. Lacan specifies, "The discourse of the unconscious is structured like a language." In his great first work, *The Interpretation of Dreams,* which is not anecdotal or superficial, as is often believed, but fundamental, Freud studied dreams' "mechanisms" or "laws," reducing their variants to two: *displacement* and *condensation.* Lacan recognized in these variants two essential figures designated by linguistics: metonymy and metaphor. Hence slips of the tongue, botched gestures, jokes, and symptoms became like the elements of the dream itself: *signifiers* inscribed in the chain of an unconscious discourse, silently (that is, deafeningly) duplicating, in the misprision of "repression," the human subject's chain of verbal discourse. Thus were we introduced to the paradox, formally familiar to linguistics, of a discourse both double and unitary, unconscious and verbal, having as its double field of deployment but a single field, with no beyond other than in itself: the field of the "signifying chain." Thus it was that the most important attainments of Saussure and the linguistics emergent from him fully entered into the understanding of the process of the discourse of the unconscious as much as of the verbal discourse of the subject, and of their relation, that is, of their nonrelation identical to their relation, in brief, of their reduplication and disjuncture. Thus it was that all the philosophical-idealist interpretations of the unconscious as a second consciousness, of the unconscious as bad faith (Sartre), of the unconscious as the cancerous survival of an archaic structure or nonsense (Merleau-Ponty), all the interpretations of the unconscious as a biological-archetypal "id" (Jung), became what they were, not the beginning of a theory, but nonexistent "theories," ideological misunderstandings.

What remained was to define (I am forced into the worst schematism, but can one avoid it in a few lines?) the meaning of the *primacy* of language's formal structure and of its "mechanisms," encountered in the practice of analytic interpretation, as itself a function of the ground of that practice: its object, that is, the present "effects" among its survivors of the forced "humanization" of the little human animal into a man or a woman. In responding to that question, it is not enough simply to invoke the pragmatic primacy of language, which is the only object and means of analytic practice. Everything that occurs in therapy is indeed played out in language (including silence, its rhythms, its scansions). But it is imperative to show in principle *why* and *how* language's empirical role in therapy, which is at once the raw material of analytic practice and the means of production of its effects (the transition, as Lacan puts it, from "empty speech" to "full speech"), is grounded in fact in analytic practice only because it is grounded *in principle* in its object, which in the last analysis grounds both that practice and its technique, and thus, since science is what we are dealing with, in the *theory* of its object.

That is, no doubt, the most original part of Lacan's work: his discovery. Lacan has shown that the passage from (in the limit case, pure) biological existence to human existence (the child of man) is effected under the Law of the Order that I will call the Law of Culture and that this Law of Culture can be conflated in its *formal* essence with the order of language. What is to be understood by this (initially) enigmatic formula? First, the *entirety of the transition* can be apprehended solely in terms of a recurrent language and designated by the language of the adult or the child *in an analytic situation*, designated, assigned, and localized under the law of language through which every human order, and thus every human role, is established. Then, within that assignment by the language of therapy surfaces the current and perpetuated presence of the absolute efficacy of the order in the very transition, of the Law of Culture in humanization.

To indicate things in a few brief words, let me note to this end the two great phases of the *transition*: (1) the moment or phase of the pre-Oedipal dual relation, in which the child, dealing only with an alter ego, the mother, who scans his life with her presence (*da*) and absence (*fort*),[3] lives this dual relation in the mode of the imaginary fascination of the ego, being himself *that* other, *some* other, *every* other, all *the others* of the primary narcissistic identification without ever being able to take, in relation to either other or self, the objectivizing distance of a third party; (2) the moment or phase of the Oedipus complex, in which a ternary structure irrupts against the ground of the dual structure, when the third party (the father) combines as an intruder with the imaginary satisfaction of the dual fascination, overthrows its economy, shatters its fascinations, and introduces the child to what Lacan calls the Symbolic Order, that of the objectivizing language that will allow him finally to say "I," "you," "he," or "she," which will thus allow the little being to situate himself as a *human child* in a world of adult thirds.

Two great moments, then: (1) that of the (pre-Oedipal) imaginary and (2) that of the symbolic (the Oedipus complex resolved), or to use a different language, that of objectivity recognized in its (symbolic) use but not yet known (the knowledge of objectivity arising at a different "age" and also from a quite different practice).

Here is the crucial point that Lacan has illuminated: those two moments are dominated, governed, and marked by a single Law, *that of the Symbolic.* The moment of the imaginary itself, which for purposes of clarity I presented a few lines earlier as preceding the symbolic and distinct from it—thus the first moment in which the child *lives* its immediate relation with a human being (the mother) without recognizing it practically as the symbolic relation that it is (that is, as the relation of a small human child with a human mother)—*is marked and structured in its dialectic by the very dialectic of the Symbolic Order*, that is, of the human order, of the human norm (the norms of the temporal rhythms of feeding, hygiene, behavioral patterns, concrete attitudes of recognition—the acceptance and refusal, yes or no, addressed to the child being only the small change, the *empirical* modalities of that constitutive Order, the Order of the Law and the Right of attribution or exclusion), in the very form of the Order of the signifier, that is, in the form of an Order formally identical to the order of language.[4]

Where a superficial or tendentious reading of Freud saw childhood only as happy and without laws, the paradise of "polymorphous perversity," a kind of state of nature scanned solely by stages of biological appearance and linked to the functional primacy of some part of the human body, the sites of "vital" (oral, anal, genital) needs,[5] Lacan shows the effectiveness of the Order, of the Law, lying in wait, from before birth, for every infant to be born and seizing on him from his very first cry to assign him to his place and role and thus his forced destination. All the stages traversed by the infant are done so under the reign of the Law, of the code of human assignment, communication, and noncommunication; his "satisfactions" bear within them the indelible and constitutive mark of the Law, of the claim of the human Law, which, like all laws, is "ignored" by no one, above all by those ignorant of it, but can be circumvented or violated by anyone, above all by its purest adherents. That is why every reduction of childhood traumas to no more than biological "frustrations" is erroneous in principle, since the Law concerning them, as a Law, sets aside all contents, exists and acts as a Law only by and within that exclusion, and the human infant receives and submits to that rule with his first breath.[6] There begins and always already began, even without any living father, what is the effective presence of the Father (who is Law) and thus of the Order of the human signifier, that is, of the Law of Culture: the discourse, the absolute condition of all discourse, the discourse present on high, that is, absent in its abyss, in every verbal discourse, the discourse of that Order, the discourse of the Other, of the great Third, who is that Order itself, the *discourse of the unconscious*. There we are given a *conceptual* hold on the *unconscious*, which is, in each human being, the absolute place in which his singular discourse seeks out its own site, seeks it, misses it, and, missing it, finds its own site, the very anchor of its site, in the imposition, imposture, complicity, and denial of its own imaginary fascinations.

That in the Oedipus complex the gendered child becomes a sexual human child (man, woman) by putting his imaginary phantasms to the test of the Symbolic and ends up, if everything "goes right," by becoming and accepting himself or herself for what he or she is: a little boy or girl among adults, having his or her child's rights in this world of adults and possessing, like every child, full *right* to one day become "like daddy," that is, a masculine human being having a wife (and no longer merely a mother), or "like mommy," that is, a feminine human being having a husband (and not merely a father)—that is but the end of the long forced march toward human childhood.

That in this ultimate drama all is played out in the matter of a previously formed language that, in the Oedipal phase, is entirely centered on and structured around the signifier *phallus*, the emblem of the Father, right, and the Law, the phantasmatic image of all Right, may seem surprising or arbitrary, but all psychoanalysts attest to it as a fact of experience.

The last phase of the Oedipus complex, "castration," conveys an idea of this. When the little boy lives and resolves the tragic and beneficent situation of castration, he accepts *not having* the same right (phallus) as his father, in particular, not having the father's right over the mother, who then reveals herself to be endowed with an intolerable status of double use, mother for the little boy and wife for the father; he gains in the process the assurance of one day having, later on, when he will have become an adult, the right that is then refused him for lack of "means." He has only a minuscule right that will become big if he himself succeeds in becoming big, having "minded his p's and q's" well. When for her part the little girl lives and assumes the tragic and beneficent situation of castration, she accepts not having the same right as her mother, that is, not yet being a woman, as her mother is. But she gains in the process, on the other hand, her own small right, that of a little girl, and the promise of a large right, the full right of a woman, when she will have become an adult, if she succeeds in growing up, by accepting the Law of Human Order, that is, submitting to it, if need be, to circumvent it—by not minding her p's and q's well.

In any event, be it in the moment of dual fascination of the Imaginary (1) or in the (Oedipal) moment of the lived recognition of insertion into the symbolic Order (2), the entire dialectic of the passage is marked in its final essence by the seal of the human Order, the Symbolic, whose *formal* laws—that is, whose *formal* concept—are furnished to us by linguistics.

Psychoanalytic theory thus can give us what makes any science not pure speculation but a science: the definition of the *formal* essence of its object, the condition of possibility of every practical and technical application to its *concrete* objects themselves. Thus psychoanalytic theory escapes the classic idealist antinomies formulated, for example, by Politzer when that author, demanding of psychoanalysis (whose revolutionary theoretical import he was the first, in France, to grasp) that it be a science of the "concrete," a true "concrete psychology," reproached it for its *abstractions*: the unconscious, the Oedipus complex, the castration complex, and so on. How can psychoanalysis claim to be the science of the *concrete* that it would and could be, Politzer asked, if it persists in *abstractions* that are but the "concrete" alienated in an abstract and metaphysical psychology? How might one join up with the "concrete" starting from such abstractions, from the abstract? In fact, no science can do without abstraction, even when it is dealing in its "practice" (which is not, observe carefully, the theoretical practice of that science but the practice of its concrete *application*) solely with those singular and unique variations constituted by the "dramas" of individuals. As Lacan thinks them in Freud—and Lacan does not think anything other than Freud's concepts, endowing them with the form of our scientificity, the only scientificity that there *is*—the "abstractions" of psychoanalysis are indeed the authentic scientific concepts of their object, to the extent that insofar as they are the concepts of their object, they contain in themselves the index, the measure, and the ground of the necessity of their abstraction, that is, the very measure of their relation to the "concrete" and thus their own relation to the concreteness of their application, commonly known as analytic practice (therapy).

Thus the Oedipus complex is not a hidden "meaning," which would be lacking only in consciousness or speech. The Oedipus complex is not a structure buried in the past that can always be restructured or transcended by "reactivating its meaning"; the Oedipus complex is the dramatic structure, the "theatrical machine,"[7] imposed by the Law of Culture on every involuntary and constrained candidate to humanity, a structure containing in itself not only the possibility but the necessity of the concrete variations in which it *exists*, for every individual who manages to reach its threshold, live it, and survive it. In its application, which is known as its practice (therapy), psychoanalysis works on the concrete "effects"[8] of those variations, that is, on the modality of the specific and absolutely idiosyncratic nodality in which the passing of the Oedipal phase was and is broached, traversed, and partially botched or eluded by this or that individual. These *variations* can be thought and known in their very essence, from within the structure of the Oedipal *invariant*, precisely because the entire transition was marked, from its inception in fascination, in its most "aberrant" forms as in its most "normal" forms, by the Law of that structure, the ultimate form of the access to the Symbolic under the very Law of the Symbolic.

I know that these brief indications not only will appear but in fact are summary and schematic and that a number of notions invoked or advanced here would require long developments to be justified or well founded. Even when illuminated in their foundation, and in the relations they maintain with the whole set of notions supporting them, even when related to the letter of Freud's analyses, they in turn pose problems: not only problems of conceptual formation, definition, and clarification but genuine new problems, necessarily produced by the development of the effort of theorization just discussed. For example, how is one to think rigorously the relation between first, the formal structure of language, the absolute condition of possibility of the existence and understanding of the unconscious, second, the concrete structures of kinship, and finally, the concrete ideological formations in which the specific functions (paternity, maternity, childhood) implied in the structures of kinship are experienced? Is it conceivable that the historical variation of those latter structures (kinship and ideology) might palpably affect one or another aspect of the instances that Freud isolated? Another question: to what extent can Freud's discovery, thought through in its rationality, by virtue of the simple definition of its object and of its site, reverberate through the other disciplines from which it distinguishes itself (such as psychology, psychosociology, sociology) and provoke in them questions about the (occasionally problematic) status of their object? Finally, a last question among so many others: what are the relations existing between analytic theory and (1) its historical conditions of emergence and (2) its social conditions of application?

(1) *Who*, then, *was Freud*, to have been able, *simultaneously*, to found analytic theory and to inaugurate, as Analyst No. 1, as the *self-analyzed*, primal father, the long line of practitioners who invoke him? (2) *Who*, then, *are psychoanalysts* to accept, *simultaneously* (and as naturally as can be), Freudian theory, the didactic tradition deriving from Freud, and the economic and social conditions (the social status of their "societies," which is closely tied to the status of the *medical* corporation or guild) in which they practice? To what extent do the historical origins and the socioeconomic conditions of the exercise of psychoanalysis reverberate through analytic technique and theory? To what extent, above all, since such is indeed the state of affairs, does the theoretical *silence* of psychoanalysts about these problems, the theoretical *repression* that these problems encounter in the analytic world, affect both analytic theory and analytic technique in their very content? Is not the eternal question of the "end of analysis," among other things, related to that repression, that is, to the *failure to think those problems*, which would be the stuff of an epistemological history of psychoanalysis and a social (and ideological) history of the analytic world?

Such are a number of genuine and truly open problems that henceforth constitute as many fields of research. It is not impossible that certain notions will emerge, in the near future, transformed by that ordeal.

That ordeal, at bottom, is the one to which Freud, in his own domain, submitted a certain traditional, juridical, moral, and philosophical (that is, in the last analysis, ideological) image of "man," of the human "subject." It was not in vain that Freud at times compared the critical repercussions of his discovery with the upheavals of the Copernican revolution. Since Copernicus, we have known that the earth is not the "center" of the universe. Since Marx, we have known that the human subject, the economic, political, or philosophical ego, is not the "center" of history—we have even known, against the philosophers of the Enlightenment and against Hegel, that history has no "center" but possesses a structure that has a necessary "center" solely in ideological misprision. Freud in turn reveals to us that the real subject, the individual in his singular essence, does not have the form of a self centered in an "ego," "consciousness," or "existence"—be it the existence of the for-itself, the body proper, or "behavior"—that the human subject is decentered, constituted by a structure that, too, has a "center" solely in the imaginary misprision of the "ego," that is, in the ideological formations in which it "recognizes" itself.

Whereby, it will have been noted, there is opened to us one of the paths by which we will perhaps one day attain a better understanding of that *structure of misprision* which is of crucial interest to all investigations of ideology.[9]

Appendix: Note to the English Edition of "Freud and Lacan"

At our request, Louis Althusser has agreed to let us reproduce the following article ["Freud and Lacan], which was written in 1964 and published in the French Communist Party [PCF] journal, *La Nouvelle Critique.*

Louis Althusser himself reckons that "there is a danger that this text will be misunderstood, unless it is taken for what it then *objectively* was: a philosophical *intervention* urging members of the PCF to recognize the *scientificity* of psychoanalysis, of Freud's work, and the importance of Lacan's interpretation of it. Hence it was polemical, for psychoanalysis had been *officially* condemned in the 1950s as 'a reactionary ideology,' and despite some modification, this condemnation still dominated the situation when I wrote this article. This exceptional situation must be taken into account when the meaning of my interpretation is assessed today."

Louis Althusser would also like to warn English readers that his article contains theses that must "*either* be corrected *or* expanded."

> In particular, in the article Lacan's theory is presented in terms that, despite all precautions, have "culturalist" overtones (whereas Lacan's theory is profoundly *anti*culturalist).
>
> On the other hand, the suggestions at the end of the article are correct and deserve a more extended treatment, that is, the discussions of the forms of *familial ideology* and the crucial role they play in initiating the functioning of the instance that Freud called "the unconscious" but that should be renamed as soon as a better term is found.
>
> This mention of the forms of familial ideology (the ideology of paternity-maternity-conjugality-infancy and their interactions) is crucial, for it implies the following conclusion—which Lacan could not express, given his theoretical formation—that is, that *no theory of psychoanalysis can be produced without basing it in historical materialism* (on which the theory of the formations of familial ideology depends, in the last instance).

Letter from Louis Althusser to Ben Brewster

February 21, 1969

2

Letters to D.

1966

DURING THE TWENTY-FIFTH *Congress of Psychoanalysts of the Romance Languages, held in Milan from May 16 to 18, 1964, René Diatkine, who was not yet Louis Althusser's psychoanalyst, delivered a paper titled "Aggressive-ness and Fantasies of Aggression," which would be published in 1966 in volume 30 of the* Revue française de psychanalyse. *After reading and extensively annotating Diatkine's text, of which an undedicated offprint has been found in his library, Louis Althusser took the opportunity in July and August 1966 to engage in an exchange of theoretical letters with the person who had already been his analyst for a year and a half.*

The documents discovered in Louis Althusser's archives, titled "Letter to D. No. 1," "D.'s Response," and "Letter to D. No. 2," are neither the originals nor copies of the letters actually sent, of which there remains no trace. All three, which were typed on the same typewriter, no doubt form part of the texts that, in The Future Lasts Forever, *Althusser claims to have had retyped by a secretary at the Ecole Normale Supérieure.[1] As with most of the writings typed in that manner—for example, the "Three Notes on the Theory of Discourses"— Althusser circulated his letters to Diatkine; his correspondence with several of his associates bears this out, without Diatkine's response ever being evoked in it.*

Since René Diatkine confirmed the reality of this exchange of letters while opposing the publication of his own text,[2] we offer here the two letters to him, restricting ourselves to summarizing the passages of Diatkine's reply necessary for an understanding of Althusser's two texts.

O.C.-F.M.

Letters to D.

Letter 1

G., 18 July 1966

I feel myself in profound agreement with—and profoundly comforted (theoretically) by—your fundamental theses, by the general *theoretical* tendency of your text, by its principal concerns, by its explicit or latent references, let us say by the *political stance adopted* (in the broad—but also in the narrow—sense) amid the theoretical problems of psycho-analysis.

I refer not merely to two or three barbs aimed at religion, to im-pertinent (that is, highly pertinent) reflections on the ideology of par-ents (you will not be forgiven the "but how can one identify with a sauce?"[1] which must already be famous . . .), on the ideological adop-tion by psychoanalysts of the "spontaneous" ideology of parents, on the more general ideology governing those reactions (a specific sen-tence about bourgeois liberals or left-wing intellectuals),[2] that is, about petty-bourgeois ideology or quite simply bourgeois ideology . . . I re-fer above all to your theses concerning *biology* and *ethology*, concerning the care you take to mark your distance unambiguously from any *biol-ogism* and any *ethologism* in the interpretation of analytic data.

On this point, which is *decisive*, you are uncompromising. In the conflicts regarding the theoretical interpretation of the facts of analy-sis, it is at present (and already has been for a long time) through this quite precise point that the *decisive dividing line* passes. Those who make the slightest theoretical concession to biology, to ethology, are *lost* for any *theoretical* reflection concerning psychoanalysis: they lapse quite quickly, if they are analysts, into *psychology* (or into culturalism, which is the "psychology" of societies), psychology, that is, the *site* of the *worst* ideological confusions and ideological perversions of our time. Understand me well: I do not mean that they cannot furnish interesting *elements* of a clinical-practical-empirical order—indeed, occasionally of a theoretical order—but these are only *elements* that must be confiscated from them since the logic of their system inevitably leads them to a *theoretical impasse,* down a path on which those who follow them can only go astray. You yourself give a striking demonstration of this with *Abraham's* myth of primitive cannibalism and its adaptation by *Melanie Klein*: the theoretical consequences are disastrous. At bottom you are quite close to saying (since you think as much) the same thing about *Nacht*:[3] his theory of aggressiveness as a reaction to "frustration" is biopsychology and nothing else; it leads nowhere, or rather, it would lead (and it leads in the case of others) to serious theoretical aberrations, if . . . Nacht did not have the good taste to have such limited talents for theory.

Against *biologism,* against its worst myths (the different forms of phylogenetic inheritance, which are invoked like so many theoretical miracles to resolve impossible problems, since they are problems poorly posed), against *ethologism* and all its variants (*psychology* and *culturalism* being at present the most dangerous), such is your basic position. I say that there is where the *decisive dividing line* passes for a theoretical labor concerning the facts of psychoanalysis (including the work of Freud). In point of fact, experience shows that it is not possible to *argue* seriously or even to *speak* with those who have remained beneath that dividing line, *even if they are analysts,* for such analysts are dominated and crushed by the ideology of biologism, ethologism, psychologism, culturalism, etc., and theoretically speaking, they are rendered *deaf* and *dumb* by it. One can argue only with those who have crossed the dividing line, for it is beyond that line that . . . salvation begins, by which I mean the realm in which theoretical reflection can begin to be exercised.

Allow me at this juncture several remarks:

(a) You will acknowledge that Lacan was the first to make clear, and in a massive, insistent, and strongly argued manner, the absolute necessity of that break with bio–etho–psycho–culturalism as the condition for all theoretical work concerning the data of psychoanalysis. For us, *from the outside,* this is quite simply a matter of objective history; it is an indisputable fact. This does not mean that *others* besides Lacan have not, for their part and in their way, discovered and recognized the same necessity, or that they will not rediscover it after him: great authors or discoverers are always accompanied, followed, and sometimes preceded by minor authors who observe the same facts and make the same discoveries. But great authors are *historically* great because they have understood the historic importance of their discovery, have made it the center of their work, and have made of that work a *public* act, *capable of modifying the theoretical situation.* By saying that they have *understood* it, I do not mean that their comprehension is necessarily to be sought in their conscious: it may be found there or not, but on the other hand, one always finds that *active* comprehension in *their work,* in the (central) place it grants their discovery, and in the *mode of existence* of that work, for example, its *public aspect,* including the *scandal* it aspires to (for whatever subjective reasons), for scandal may also be objectively the index of an effect having a historic import.

I am saying this for us, but also for you. It may be that every member of the audience of your society, hearing you struggle against bio-etho-psychology, *realized* that you were taking up, in a very personal manner, Lacan's fundamental argument and fundamentally what we *owe* him *historically* in the sense I previously defined. But I am not absolutely sure of it. I have grounds for believing that most of your listeners, or at least certain—and not the least—of them, are carefully *repressing* (and in the sense not of analytic repression but of ideologico-political repression) the existence of Lacan and his contribution, which is on this point *absolutely decisive.* Such repression is, allow me to say, *unhealthy.* Even if it is, and all the more if it is, apparently justified by the "political" precautions that need be taken with individuals as eminent as Nacht *who lapse into psychology.* One cannot allow oneself *theoretical compromises,* for one always pays extremely dearly for them. You extricate yourself in your text by a *half-measure;* you are prudent but at bottom *quite clear* about Nacht. On the other hand, you don't speak about Lacan. (You quote him, but with regard to another question.)[4] In the long term, and even in the short and middle term, this policy of silence is and cannot but be *bad politics.* Were it only for the reason I already gave you: your silence is the surest means by which Lacan keeps you *prisoner* of his fascination and his personal quirks, at the very moment when you believe you have broken (and he too believes you have broken) all ties with him. As long as you will not have openly, publicly, objectively, and demonstratively, that is, theoretically, clarified your dealings with him—and to clarify one's dealings with someone means *to begin by acknowledging what one owes him*—he will have a "hold" *on you*, and with that hold, he prevents you simultaneously from being theoretically *free* and from advancing in theoretical research.

There is in this something that goes very far and about which you once spoke to me concerning analysts' tendency to "interpret" in terms of drives, etc., every initiative taken by an analyst in the domain of argument or theoretical research (the organization of meetings, public speaking, etc.). I wonder whether *you* are not (*you* = analysts in general, including the best intentioned, the very best, thus including yourself, R.D.) to a certain extent victim of what you (R.D.) were telling me so recently. In shunning or avoiding the *objective* (politico-theoretical) task of clearly settling accounts with Lacan, you are *behaving* as though everything transpiring between you and Lacan were subject exclusively to analytic interpretation (his attitude, on the one hand, yours, on the other). In not making (*in your acts* and secondarily in your consciousness) the indispensable *distinction* between, say, what is in the order of historical and *theoretical objectivity*, on the one hand, and what is in the order of *individual drives*, on the other, *you subject yourselves* to the effects of those drives, by which I mean, to put it crudely, solely to the "staged" effects of Lacan—and you are *paralyzed* in the face of his theoretical work when confronting the *objectively* valid aspects of what his very "style" has achieved: his theoretical *oeuvre*, within which, to be sure, one must be selective, but when you have sent the greengrocer packing, it's no longer possible to select one's tomatoes!

To take things still further, I believe that when you (you in the collective sense: analysts in their relation with Lacan, whatever that relation may be, since one can generalize) deliver yourselves over to those drives, in the sense we have just seen, *in reality* you are delivering yourselves over to what (I was about to say for all eternity!) has been stretching its arms out to you, while exploiting those subjective appearances: a certain *ideology* of compromise in which you take refuge and in which you are able to take refuge because it has always been at your disposition, within reach, the *empiricist* ideology with all the grave consequences it entails concerning the effects it implies for your relations with theory.

All this may seem to be enigmatic. I hope to clarify it in what follows.

(b) And first of all by a second observation. Taking your distance, as you do, from every bio-etho-psychologism is a crucial condition for all theoretical work, but it is an entirely *negative* condition. It teaches you that one *must not* seek an understanding of analytic data in biology, ethology, psychology, etc.; it teaches you that psychoanalytic data are *irreducibly different* (and you say it quite well), but all that remains *negative* and *programmatic*. The enabling condition of theoretical work is not theoretical work; the condition on the basis of which theoretical concepts may be defined does not give us the beginning of the content of those theoretical concepts. In those circumstances we are in the case of what I have called "practical concepts"[5] (deep within theory, to be sure), that is, *concepts indicative of direction*: one must go not this way but that way . . . advance in this direction if you want to have the possibility of finding something valid, etc. But all the actual work remains to be done. I say this for formal reasons since I know that you are aware of it, and infinitely more than I am.

(c) And yet we have here in short order an example in which things get more specific, in other words, in which absolute theoretical rejections (of bio-etho-psychologism), which have until this point had but a *negative* content, acquire a *positive* content from the theoretical point of view. I am thinking of your theoretical thesis concerning the difference in *status* between what transpires, say, "in" or "with" the child during *the first month*, on the one hand, and what one may think transpires *later on*, at a time that you don't specify with any precision but whose undeniable signs in any event knock one's eyes out as of the eighth month.[6]

That thesis allows you to render unto Caesar what is Caesar's and to fix, *within the development of the child*, the site of the decisive *dividing line* between the bio-etho-psychological, on the one hand, and the psychoanalytic, on the other. It is clear; it plainly corresponds to experience, to indisputable facts. It allows the rights of biology to be acknowledged even as they are *restricted* in time. There is a beneath and a beyond. Don't make me say what I am not saying, that after the limit there is *no longer* anything biological, ethological, etc. Of course these factors subsist, but at the time of the limit something radically *new* has emerged, let's say, to be brief, *the unconscious,* which did not exist prior to the limit. This means that *before* that limit, it was the *exclusive* realm of the bio-etho, etc. This is what I call rendering unto Caesar what is Caesar's.

This is clear, and it provides satisfaction or may provide satisfaction to everyone, including the biologists, the ethologists, and the psychologists themselves, provided that they not be too contentious or addled. It also restores some order to the biological ravings of Abraham and Melanie and other cruder deviations of contemporary psychoanalysis. It is, then, also a source of satisfaction *to you too.*

And yet I should like to note here—and thus to raise a question—that I believe your thesis to be much more an *illustration* of the polemical necessity of locating an absolute line of demarcation than a *demonstration* of the form that this break or limit might take or should take in the theoretical domain. In other words, and to go to the heart of matters, I fear that it is an *ideological illusion* to want to *inscribe* that dividing line, with a bio-ethological *before* and an *after* in which something radically *new* (the unconscious) figures *in the very development of the child.*

I will explain myself in moving on to my second point. But I was obliged to mention in my first point that consequence to the extent that it is, in my opinion, a *conclusion falsely drawn from correct premises.* Falsely drawn because the correct premises are only *negatively* correct, and the falsity of the consequences drawn is a function of the fact that no account has been taken of this *negative* status of their correctness, that one has not *criticized in its foundation* what one was *rejecting,* the result being that at the moment of passing from the negative to the theoretical positive, one unwittingly *relapses* into what one has just *rejected,* and that the combination of that *rejection* and that *acceptance* (provoked by that relapse) has yielded what it could not but yield: a *theoretical compromise* arranged between what one meant and what one refused to say, a compromise that takes the classical form of a division of territory, with a *border,* the form of a "render unto Caesar what is Caesar's," render unto the pure bio-ethological what is the pure bio-ethological's, the child's first month. A before and an after: a "this side of the Pyrenees" and a "beyond the Pyrenees." All of which *demonstrates that there are* Pyrenees, and everyone is happy.

But all this is possible, I shall attempt to demonstrate, only because you are *silent* on what has been said by Lacan, who even if he says nonsense, and through his very nonsense, *knows* that theoretical compromise must not be accepted and says it, does not stop saying it, knows that one can not divide a territory, knows, finally, that an illustration is an illustration and not a demonstration. Be kind enough to acknowledge that I am speaking of Lacan solely from the theoretical and historical point of view. To be sure, I could choose not to speak of him at all and present to you what I am about to say without mentioning his name. But that would amount to hiding one's head in the sand, for Lacan exists and has produced an oeuvre of considerable weight, whether it be acknowledged or repressed. To speak about him is also to begin establishing the wherewithal for making certain choices within his work and for getting it into one's head that there are *imperative criteria* of selection—that is, of epistemological and ideological criticism—and thus that one cannot begin dividing things up at random.

(2) I come then to your theoretical thesis, or rather to the *one* of your critical theses that appears to me to be simultaneously the most important and the most subject to caution, *at least in the form* you have given it.

Finally, after having (quite properly) written that "it may be arbitrary to situate the origin of abscissa at birth" (we may wonder what the positive meaning of that sentence is; see my later comments),[7] you nonetheless insist (and in your very refusal to situate it at birth) on the concept of the "*origin* of abscissa," that is, you insist all the same on elaborating a "genesis" (cf. p. 73, "the genesis of fantasies" that you have attempted with Lebovici in your Rome presentation of 1953).[8] I don't want to take you *literally*, that is, to take your word for a *theoretical concept.* You are aware that I consider the concepts of *origin* and *genesis* as fundamentally religious—when taken, of course, in the rigorous sense constituted by their *couple.* This is an opinion that I have sustained with arguments that were already serious in the preface to *Reading "Capital"* and that seem to me increasingly well founded and increasingly demonstrable. When you use the concepts of origin and genesis, you do not (thank God!) make rigorous—that is, religious—use of them, but you *do not quite* escape that usage and its effects. I would like to demonstrate that.

I shall say things in a very schematic and crude manner to get to what is essential.

Your thesis contains, in fact, two distinct propositions that are absolutely different in essence and that nonetheless are found side by side and occasionally conflated.

First Proposition. This is the idea that something irreducible *irrupts* in the human child, by which is to be understood something irreducible to the biological, the ethological. You *illustrate* that prodigiously accurate and fruitful idea in ten different ways. By showing that at the level of *empirical observation,* one is dealing not only with different mechanisms in the animal and the child but also with different mechanisms in the child during the first month and, let's say, the eighth. By showing that the *reality* of the primal scene is not necessary for the fantasy of a primal scene to irrupt and function, and similarly for other fantasies. By showing that the child who has "never" been the object of aggression nonetheless always produces fantasies of aggression (you return on several occasions to that "central question," and rightly so).

That set of examples and arguments allows you to pursue two ends: (1) to demonstrate the specificity of psychoanalysis and particularly of Freudian concepts (at least those that register that specificity) in relation to biologizing and ethologizing concepts; and (2) to show at work a very peculiar dialectic, one that is not that of a *genesis* (since it is impossible to deduce the unconscious from the biological or the ethological, be it animal or human) but that of an *irruption*: something *new* begins to *function in an autonomous manner.*

Everything relating in your text to that first proposition is *extremely fruitful,* and I quite admired, among other things, the technical consequences that you derive from it for the conduct of therapy; your entire theory of the *meshing* and *unmeshing* of drives, the *conjuncture* and *divergence* (the perversions) of drives, and a whole array of particularly felicitous formulations (the intemporality of the unconscious, p. 46, among others).

I will not conceal from you that I am quite interested in these forms, which seem to me to be the forms of a true *dialectic,* quite opposed, or rather completely foreign, to the forms of Hegelian or vulgar dialectic, which for its part rests on the idea of a *genesis-origin.* But I am interested in them also because these new forms are indispensable for all theoretical work on analytic data—your text is convincing proof of it. It is when you utilize these concepts, this new dialectic, that your concepts "adhere" best to experience, that is, to the psychoanalytic data that you furnish.

Second Proposition. But along with the first your thesis contains a second proposition, which is far less established theoretically and thus vulnerable to criticism.

One can acquire an idea of that second proposition by assembling a whole series of themes, concepts, and arguments that you employ and by confronting them with a certain number of pertinent silences.

I shall note first of all that you are openly against biology and ethology (in the sense that we have seen), but on another score, you are infinitely more indulgent toward *psychology*. You even use the word on several occasions positively in your own name, such as when you speak of the "greater psychological complexity" of the child's behavior, etc. And above all you make use of extremely dubious psychological-philosophical concepts ("living experience," "meaning," "intentionality," "human experience," etc.). To be sure, you make use of them in passing, and that entails no *direct* consequences in your analyses. But if one aligns the right you arrogate to utilize psychological or phenomenological concepts (phenomenology is the religious psychology of our time) without criticizing them with the fact that *nowhere* do you denounce, by explicitly naming it, the *psychologizing* temptation, which is at least [as] dangerous for psychoanalysis as is the *biologizing* tendency (if not more so), that alignment may become pertinent. To be sure, there is in your text all one might require for psychology to be entirely condemned, since it is only *ethology*, and ethology is condemned, but it is the reader who is obliged to draw that conclusion on his own. You yourself do not draw it. This is not only, I am convinced, for political reasons, because Nacht is extremely tainted by psychologism or because he is not happy taking on psychologists frontally (which remains to be seen), but for deeper reasons, which we will find on another level.

It is because at bottom you don't *quite* relinquish the idea of a *genesis* (the idea of genesis is one of the *organic* concepts of every psychology). I do not know what your communication at Rome in 1953 contains on the subject of the genesis of fantasies.[9] But one can find traces of this concept of genesis in places other than where it is *explicitly* mentioned: quite precisely in certain passages of your analysis and in certain silences or significant omissions in this respect, for one can say that in such places the concept of genesis aspires to *realization* and in fact, to a certain extent, succeeds in being realized (to a certain extent only because that realization is thwarted by all the positive and fertile concepts that I have related to your *first proposition*). I shall take only a few examples. It is clear that the difficulty you experience in *dating* the *moment* in which there irrupts in the child's history the new structure that interests psychoanalysis (and that has nothing to do with the structures that psychology decrees *psychological*, however "complex" they may be) is indicative of your theoretical hesitation, quite precisely of the contradiction existing between the *nongenesis* required by your radical distinction between the biological and the unconscious and the properly ideological and, say, *psychological* (or rather psychologizing) need to constitute, *nevertheless, a genesis*. You argue from within that contradiction, or rather, you *dodge* it, *avoid* it with propositions (p. 75, last paragraph; p. 79, paragraphs 9 and 10; p. 82, first paragraph; etc.) that are no more than descriptive and vague ("however, this situation evolves rapidly . . . ," "this modification of the relational system of the child . . . ," "thus are created the necessary conditions for the appearance of language . . . ," etc.). These descriptive propositions are in need of theoretical concepts to exist, for example, the concept of "evolution," the concept of "relational system of the child," etc. But those concepts are not good and can even be bad (evolution is a theoretical concept of biology; relational system is a theoretical concept of psychology, not psychoanalysis). In point of fact, you are unable to *date* the moment of the irruption, and that is a good thing. But you give the feeling that one ought *to be able to date it*, at least in principle, and thus to inscribe a border correlative to a genesis. There must indeed be a relation of genesis between before and after if there is a before and an after—I mean, if there is a biological before and an unconscious after.

That same genetic temptation appears in a curious definition of the unconscious as *memory*, which plainly obsesses you ("mnemic reserve," "memory," etc.), even as you simultaneously give a theoretically irreproachable definition of the "atemporality of the unconscious." If we say that the unconscious is a memory, we lapse back into one of the worst concepts of psychology(!), and we are tempted to think that memory = history, that therapy = rectified rememoration = correct historicity, that curing a neurosis means restoring it to its "historicity,"[10] which is surely one of the least felicitous formulas to have emerged from Lacan's pen. As you see, from memory to history the path is short, and from psychology to phenomenology, the path is just as short, since it's the same one. Moreover, the path toward psychology is never so short as when one has never left psychology, which confirms a famous proverb: "to return home, all you need is the right address, your own," which might be modified as follows: "to be sure of returning home, a good method: never leave it."

(It seems to me that the unconscious is no more a memory than is absolutely any *functioning mechanism*, including the most advanced cybernetic mechanisms. On that, if my "memory" is correct, there are some rather good things in Lacan.)

Still on the same order, that is, concerning your *second proposition*, I come to an even more impressive *silence* in your text. Its subject is quite precisely *language*.

This is no doubt the most theoretically important point: *the theoretical crossroads*, from the point of view of your own thought.

See your paragraph 10: "Thus are created the conditions necessary for the appearance of language . . . the child can take an interest in the signified by way of the signifier solely *on the condition that he retain an elementary memory* of the feared or cherished lost object" (p. 79). You take up the same theme on p. 82: "the child is brought to discover what is beyond his immediate sensory world thanks to the play of that *mnemic reservoir* which is his *unconscious* in the process of formation *and to take an interest* in the signified by way of the signifier, that is, in human language" (my emphasis).

In these texts I am all the same obliged to take you at your word, for your words, even taking account of the fact that your work does not allow you the indispensable time needed for polishing concepts, plainly have *weight for you*, and their systematic conjunction clearly has *a theoretical meaning*, the very one you are intent on uttering.

In these two crucial passages one in fact observes the "appearance"—as you say (it's the *proper* word)—of *language*, which means that before that moment, it had passed or remained unnoticed! The mother, the father, the stranger (the nonmother of which the father is a variation that will become concretized as a father), the whole elementary kinship *structure*, then—followed by elements of parental (and above all *maternal) ideology*—had *effectively appeared in our analysis; but language, no.* You make it "*appear*" only when the child begins to speak! I believe there is here a *factual* omission (the fact of the existence of language: father and mother speak, are speaking beings, even garrulous ones! even when they are silent, perhaps above all when they are silent) that constitutes a *theoretical* omission whose consequences are important. All the same, you don't speak about the father solely when the child begins to *become a father* (at age twenty or thirty) or a mother!

And yet you speak of language *only when the child begins to become an animal loquax!!* I shall return to that theoretical omission.

But let's look at another important detail in these two passages. You say and *say again* that the appearance of language in the child is conditioned by the disposition of a *memory,* and you say that this memory is unconscious. I am not saying that this is false, but I can't help noting that you think of the unconscious as a *memory* for theoretical reasons that may be hidden but that are clear, all the same, because the concept of memory *takes the place of,* represents the equivalent of, a *genesis* that you want to be neither biological nor ethological, but a genesis nevertheless, and one that ends up being thought out in a register about which you do not speak: psychology (the concept of memory is a fundamental concept of psychology). The problem is that since you in fact made language *disappear* from all your preceding analyses, you can obviously make it "*appear*" at the convenient moment (when it effectively "appears" in the child), but you pay a high price for the facility of that arrangement, which is, moreover, a relative confusion (the child's language, at least at the outset, is not identical to language per se), for you are obliged to have us witness, like our classical authors of the eighteenth century and our contemporary psychologists, who are their theoretical heirs, *the genesis of language from memory!* This comes close to being vintage Condillac, and I don't say it in mockery, but it cannot be Freud. This does not mean that the *irruption* of the child's symbolic language (which is objective in its conformity to the code defining social language) does not raise a theoretical problem; it means that one is sure not to resolve it by posing it in terms of *a psychological genesis* (language as a consequence of memory), quite precisely by having taken pains to make *language disappear* as a structural element, if not as the essential structure of the parental "milieu" and of what "occurs" between the mother and the child, before his birth, then after, etc. The problem of the irruption of the child's language is not a problem of genesis but above all a problem of the *reproduction* of an *already existent language* in the very milieu in which the child "appears." This suggests that the manner in which you pose the problem raises numerous difficulties. You indeed say that the child goes toward the signified by way of the signifier, but this signifier is a *memory,* and the memory of an "*object*" whose status is divided between two meanings that are, however, quite distinct (the objective mother and the-mother-for-the-child, say, the phantasmatic mother). To say that this signifier is a memory is to incline toward psychologism. And yet, *at the same time,* you avoid psychologism by showing that this memory functions in a specific manner, *like a code,* with specific *binary-ternary* correlations (binary: absence/presence of the mother; ternary: mother/nonmother/father). At the same time, however, as you bring into relief that what is important is not the genesis but the *structural functioning* of this binary-ternary coded system, you can't resist the wish to ground this system in its own *genesis,* that of the child's *experience* of the discontinuity of the mother's presence and absence—and there we are at the threshold of that *psychology* from which you have nonetheless just offered proof (in what you say about the coded system) that you want to carefully keep your distance.

(d) All this, it seems to me, might be summarized as follows: you want to avoid *psychologism,* and your experimental practice (the psychiatric or clinical observation of children, as well as your analytic practice) obliges you to do so constantly, since you are well aware that the *coded system* begins to function all of a sudden and irrupts, despite great variations in the conditions of childhood *experience* (see what you say, luminously, about the appearance of aggressive fantasies *outside of any experience of aggression*!). And yet you don't manage to avoid recourse to psychologism, or at least the temptation of recourse to it, the temptation of a *genesis,* the use of *psychological* concepts (the unconscious as memory! the genesis of language from memory! the genesis of the mother-signifier from the *experience* of her alternating absence and presence!). All this for reasons that, to be sure, may be a function of our present ignorance but that are *also* a function (since ignorance is not a theoretical argument) of the fact that you have quite simply omitted, shunted to the side, or repressed (theoretically!) an important element in the dossier: *language*—not the child's language, but the language that the child does no more than *adopt* when he finally begins to speak. Now we may assume that this "character" named language plays a very important role in that performance in which the child must at any cost *discover* his own (his unfindable role).

How is one to understand this *theoretical omission,* which corresponds to the omission of a *fact,* of a given, of an indisputable element of the reality in which the child is *caught* from the time of his birth? Now it happens that—in a manner one might criticize or rectify—Lacan did not omit that *element* and that he *has taken it seriously.* I do not contest that some of the conclusions he has drawn from this may be wrong, but it is not by *omitting* an element that may play a crucial role or that, if it does not play a crucial role, at least plays an important role, that one can rectify this or that erroneous conclusion drawn by Lacan. When one has quite simply eliminated the premises, there is no longer any conclusion at all to rectify.

I rediscover here, concerning that precise question, the problem of your *theoretical* relations with Lacan's work. I say *theoretical* (and not personal) relations and Lacan's *work* (and not Lacan). And once again what I am saying about it has meaning only on the *theoretical* level and in no way affects all the psychoanalytic data you furnish, their description, the understanding of their mechanisms, nor even this or that extremely pertinent theoretical concept that you propose to account for the facts of analysis. I am speaking from a *strategic theoretical* point that may be detected as such in your own thinking, through your very *silence,* when it is a question of *language.* It is a question that you *cannot dodge* if you want to "advance" psychoanalytic theory, and it is a question that you cannot resolve, as you are tempted to do, through recourse to "psychology," which, moreover, you have every reason (in the very logic of your theoretical attitude) to *reject.* Now that question has been *posed* by Lacan in definite terms. He is about the only one to have posed it; in any event, he was the first to have done so in the analytic world, and he posed the question as a *decisive question.* You may disagree with his answers to that question, but you cannot proceed as though he had not raised it and as though the answers he gives do not exist. Even if his work needs correction, Lacan's theoretical work exists, and *one cannot not take it into account.* What would you say of a physicist who for one reason or another would (theoretically) repress the theoretical work of Einstein in its entirety and, taking none of it into account, would attempt to fabricate his own theory of physics based on the problems of pre-Einsteinian physics? It would be absurd, not merely because he would lose a considerable amount of time in the process, but because theoretical discoveries not being merely a matter of *time,* he would risk not finding anything! I know that my analogy is *disproportionate,* but I make it so deliberately to give you, as in a mirror, an idea of the *disproportionate* character of the distance you are taking in relation to Lacan's work.

Let me be understood. Lacan's claim and his unique originality in the world of psychoanalysis lie in his being a *theoretician.* Being a theoretician does not mean producing a theoretical concept corresponding to an empirical, clinical, practical fact, or even *several* theoretical concepts; it means producing a *general system* of theoretical concepts, rigorously articulated with each other and capable of accounting for the *total set* of facts and of the field of analytic practice. This ambition is *in itself* perfectly legitimate; I would even say it is vital, absolutely indispensable for making of psychoanalysis something other than a practice capable of finding its bearings practically among its objects, its domain, and its procedures but *theoretically mute* (incapable in particular of situating itself and its object within the field of different extant sciences). Making psychoanalysis the object of that theorization is extremely important for analytic practice itself. I realize that you agree with all these points. *In principle*, then, Lacan's ambition is well founded and excellent, and it deserves to be acknowledged publicly and openly, since outside of Lacan, *who* can truly say that he has that *ambition* and that he has embodied it in an oeuvre? *No one.* I recall that I refer to theoretical ambition in the precise sense defined at the beginning of this paragraph. And I say, repeat, and maintain, and it's a point on which no compromise is possible, because it would amount quite simply to denying reality—I say that at least in France (but I am convinced that my remark is valid without restriction), *outside of Lacan, there is at present no one.*

This declaration will shock, but it is true. For it is one thing to have such an ambition subjectively and [another] to have embodied it *objectively* in a body of work, whatever its shortcomings may be. And it is one thing to have produced this or that concept, or a group of concepts (a number of intelligent psychoanalysts have achieved this, and this is already quite good), and another to have produced a *general system of rigorously articulated concepts,* for that is what really makes a theoretician. If you are willing to accept these criteria, which are perfectly objective (they are valid for all scientific disciplines without exception), my conclusion is unassailable: *outside of Lacan, there is at present no one.*

And if that is how things are, one must draw the appropriate consequences and not hide one's head under the table. One must first of all recognize what is and acknowledge the *level* at which Lacan is situated (the *level of the theoretical* at which he functions is vital, independent of the validity of one or another of his theses). One must then *elevate oneself to that level*, and to do so, one must *make use of the work* already accomplished by Lacan to attain that level—if not, it's the madness of repressing what already exists for the pleasure of . . . what? Reinventing it? It is on that condition, when one is at that level and has made use of the work furnished by Lacan to elevate oneself to it, that one can begin *settling scores* with Lacan and, if need be, for at that point it becomes *possible* and *indispensable*, call him to account for a certain number of errors, if such be the case, which includes criticizing the *terms* in which he has posed the problem of theorizing analytic practice and its data. I insist on this: to be able to criticize the terms in which he has posed this problem, one must first of all acknowledge *that he has posed the problem* and acknowledge all the (theoretical) conditions he had to satisfy and that you must satisfy to be able to reach the *level* at which it becomes *possible to pose the problem*. It is only at that point that a genuine theoretical critique becomes possible, *not before*. One has to know this. Take the example of language. You encounter that question, which is extremely difficult, in your very practice, and you attempt to deal with it simultaneously through an *elision* (silence on language as a constitutive structure of the familial "milieu") and through a *psychological genesis*; at the same time, however, since you are a good "empiricist" who accounts for the facts, you say *something different* by speaking of a binary-ternary coded system, but *you do not theoretically assume* that *other thing*. Lacan, for his part, does so from the outset. He may err in the *manner* in which he poses the problem, but he does not err *in posing the problem of language at the theoretical level*. But you, you *don't pose* the problem of language at the theoretical level. All you manage to say against this or that thesis of Lacan's will remain *without theoretical effect*, even if your critique is correct, as long as you do not situate your critique at the very *level* at which Lacan *is right* to pose the problem of language. There is where your "empiricism" costs you dearly, for you are well aware that a "fact" cannot upset a theory (if that theory is not a pure delusion): *to upset* (and, at the limit, replace) *a theory*, the "fact" has to *become* theory, that is, be conceived at the *theoretical level*, in a system of theoretical concepts. The entire history of the sciences proves it. He who attacks a true theory with a simple *theoretically* unelaborated "fact" attacks a fortress with a slingshot.

I thus ask you afresh the question I have already asked you: why do you allow yourself to *repress* the work of Lacan in this manner? It's an error, a mistake, the mistake you must not commit and that you are nevertheless committing. You will answer me with the individual Lacan, but that is not what is at stake: it is a matter of his work, and even beyond his work, it is a matter of that of which it is the sole extant proof: it is a matter of the *existence* in principle of theory in the field of psychoanalysis. Paris was well worth a mass: between the two of us, the "individual" Lacan, his "style" and his idiosyncrasies and all the effects they have produced, including the personal wounds, all that "*is well worth theory.*" There are some goods for which one never pays too dearly, the very ones that bring more than they cost. That it is difficult, demanding, testing, that it calls for courage and lucidity, a great deal of courage and lucidity, and even sacrifices, is certain, but "theory" is well worth that. And yet I want to add one more thing. In my view it is not only for historical reasons (breaks) or personal ones ("impossible" re-lations with Lacan) that you are repressing his work in this way. It is in the last analysis for reasons having to do with *the idea you have of theory* and its relation with practice and the data of experience, with the idea, then, that you have of the nature and role of theory. You have uttered with a good deal of modesty, with lucidity, with a good deal of lucid-ity and courage and far too much modesty, a phrase I would like to take up: "I am an empiricist." You are one in the most noble and au-thentic sense, but you are *also* one (and this is not your doing; it is an almost inevitable *effect* of the state not merely of the training given fu-ture physicians, of the one given future analysts, but also of the "human sciences" in their entirety) in the *ideological* sense. Ideological empiri-cism is a certain *falsified* conception of the relation of theory to expe-rience and consequently of the nature of theory and its role. It is the "spontaneous" ideology of all practitioners, whatever their practice, even if it be largely theoretical. That is where we are all *at*, and it is from there that we must all *part in order to achieve a distance from it.* This is the case, as you know, not only in the field of your discipline, or in other disciplines that are quite scientific and formalized, but in politics as well. We have all to free ourselves from the empiricist ideology, which dominates us without our realizing it. It is thus a very good sign that you declare yourself to be an "empiricist," for I see in it the promise that you will soon be wringing the neck of empiricist *ideol-ogy*, which is the greatest obstacle possible when one wants to accede to theory. No longer subject to empiricist ideology, you will not lose that extraordinary *scientific empiricism* that constitutes your exceptional strength and merit, that scientific empiricism that carries you, despite your psychologizing temptations, into the question of language, to the very threshold of theory. *That* empiricism, scientific empiricism, will produce other astonishing effects once you clear the immense space lying before it and that is at present still blocked by the elements of *ideological* empiricism that I believe I detect in certain of your moves, in certain of your silences, including your repression of Lacan's work. On that day the question of your relations with Lacan's work will be resolved, I believe I can say, by itself, in any event without the (serious) shadow of those (personal, historical, "social") difficulties that currently are literally "blocking your view."

(e) A final point. I return to the question of the insertion of the dividing line (between the biological and the unconscious) *within* the temporality of the history of the child's development.

It seems to me that I would be able to make myself better understood by saying that to want at any cost *to inscribe* at a precise moment (or more loosely, as you do, between the beginning of the second and the end of the eighth month) *within* the time of the child's development that dividing line is to yield to an *ideological* illusion of a *psychologistic* nature. For it amounts to relapsing into the bio-ethologist ideology that you criticize so well on another front: it is to believe that one can assign *within* what is *then* declared to be purely biological (the *before* of the irruption of the unconscious) the origin, birth, irruption of the nonbiological, the unconscious. *Whether you want it or not*, it entails implementing in a defined manner terms whose disposition *cannot not induce the position of a problem of genesis.* Once that *before* has been implemented, and that *after*, you will proceed and speak in vain, for you have set up a *logic* that impels you naturally to pose the problem of the genesis of the *after* from the *before.* You will defend yourself in vain against that logic and its effects, for you cannot quite escape it. *It has you in its grip,* and the proof is that you want to elaborate a *genesis*; since you don't want to elaborate a biological genesis, you in fact produce a *psychological* genesis *despite your precautions* (and it is not by accident that you produce a *psychological* genesis, since you quite significantly *spared psychology* in the course of your major critique of the theoretical deviations toward biologism and ethologism!). In my telling you that, you will see that I too *interpret* what one might be tempted to call your ideologico-theoretical *unconscious.* I would have many reservations to make on those *terms*, since I believe that is not possible to speak of an ideological unconscious. In any event, that "unconscious" (which I would call by a different name, but never mind) exists, and *it should not be confused with the psychoanalytic unconscious.* If we are in agreement, it is the obvious condition of a theoretical exchange of this sort: it is situated at the level of ideological and theoretical criticism, and not at the level of the interpretation of "unconscious" psychoanalytical mechanisms.

I am of the opinion, then, that the *project* of wanting to inscribe that dividing line *within* the child's developmental history (which plainly has considerable *polemical* effectiveness, since it keeps the biologists behind the dividing line . . .) is quite definitively a *psychologistic* and thus an *ideological* project. I believe that you have yielded to it unwittingly, under the sway of the mechanisms of the ideological "unconscious," quite precisely as an effect of the complex mechanisms of empiricist ideology, acting on your (well-founded) rejection of biologism and ethologism. The "compromise" I was speaking about thus results from the combination of the effects of (unconscious) empiricist ideology and your (conscious and nonideological) rejection of biologism and ethologism. This "compromise" has a name: it is a *genesis* that remains at bottom psychological.

It is thus imperative to pose the problem differently, and, even as one rejects every biologism or ethologism, not attempt to assign a *temporal origin* within the child's development to that unconscious that you so remarkably dub "atemporal." A difficult position to maintain, and in any event less comfortable from the perspective of the polemic against biologism and ethologism, less immediately "profitable"—but a theoretically more accurate position and consequently a more fertile one in the long run. This is in general terms Lacan's position, even if, once again, one may think that the *terms* in which he defines that position can or should be *rectified*. But there too, a possible rectification of terms can occur only on the condition that one previously acknowledges the *correctness in principle* of that position. You will not be surprised to rediscover, among the terms defining that position, in the first rank, *language* (among other terms). I suggest simply that it may be from language that its "atemporality" comes to the unconscious, and indeed a bit more than that "atemporality": the fact that it is the *unconscious* (it being understood that the unconscious is not only *unconscious*) and the fact that it "functions" under definite *laws* that Freud already identified as being those of language. One must advance down that path with caution, I openly agree, but *currently* I am not convinced that we dispose of any other *path* on which to advance.

"LETTER TO D. NO. 1" is followed by a reply by D. dated August 13, 1966, and written in Crete. Since René Diatkine has opposed our publishing his text, we

summarize here the several elements of the reply necessary for understanding Althusser's second letter to D.

D. notes first that Althusser's first letter is based on the following two postulates: "the unconscious is structured like a language"; "the child is caught in language from the time of his birth." His answer is then articulated in three points:

1. The comparison with language would be insufficient to account for the totality of mechanisms of the unconscious. According to Diatkine, if the relation conscious-preconscious/unconscious is on the order of the relation signified/signifier, it is insufficient for defining the unconscious.

2. Even if the child perceives from the outset the sonorities of language, it is abusive to say that he is "caught in language from the time of his birth." Language is indeed the organizing principle of the "secondary processes," but it actually intervenes only after the establishment of a binary system (good-bad, present-absent) that will furnish a ground for Oedipal triangulation. One cannot speak of an "influence of language from the time of birth," since "communication through language necessitates the confrontation of a child already endowed with a history with adults who, to be sure, have their own."

3. The atemporality of the unconscious does not prevent it from irrupting "within time": there is a "before" and there is an "after." While declaring himself ready to renounce the word genesis, Diatkine submits that the vocabulary of diachrony is inevitable and that Althusser himself does not escape it when he affirms that "something new begins to function in an autonomous manner." In those conditions, and since it is impossible to psychoanalyze a child before language mastery has been achieved, it is indispensable to revert to "direct observation"—which it is possible to do by avoiding the traps of ethology.

Letter 2

G., 22 August 1966

(1) Concerning genesis.

I will begin by this concept, about which I feel a bit more assured.

Since no concept exists in isolation, or, to adapt a line from Marx, who says that solitude exists only in society, since every isolated concept exists only within a conceptual society, to delve into the concept of genesis means to delve into the conceptual society in which it exists, the concepts that are organically related to it or, if you prefer, its theoretical "connotations." It is plainly a matter not of mere philology or etymology but of a theoretical semantic field, not of a semantic field definable a priori, but of the actual semantic field in which the concept of genesis—as it is *practiced*, used, and manipulated—is inscribed. It is within that actually existent, empirically existent, and controllable field that I shall use the following expression: whoever says genesis says . . .

Whoever says genesis says the reconstitution of the process through which a phenomenon A has actually been *engendered*. That reconstitution is itself a process of knowledge: it has meaning (as knowledge) only if it *reproduces* (reconstitutes) the real process that *engendered* phenomenon A.

You will see immediately that whoever says genesis says from the outset that the process of *knowledge* is *identical* in all its parts and in their order of succession to the actual process of engendering. That means that the process of knowledge is in all respects and for all purposes immediately *superimposable* on the real or actual process of engendering. That means, to speak in less abstract terms, that whoever elaborates the genesis of a phenomenon A can *follow the tracks*, in all its phases, *from the origin* of the actual process of engendering without any interruption, that is, without any discontinuity, lacuna, or break (the words hardly matter).

This *immediate* and total overlap, without any interruption of actual process by the process of knowledge, *implies* the idea, which seems to be a matter of course, that the subject of the real or actual process is a single and same *subject, identifiable* from the origin of the process to the end.

Here I am merely casting light on the implications of the effective use of the concept of genesis, or on the implications of its practice.

Whoever says genesis is thus implementing, with necessary organic unity, the following concepts:

the process of *engendering*,

the *origin* of the process,

the *end* or term of the process (phenomenon A), and

the *identity* of the *subject* of the process of engendering.

If one inquires into the *meaning* constituted by the system of those concepts, one observes that it refers massively to a "model," that is, to an "experience" impregnating the system of concepts and their organization. That experience is that of *generation*, whether it be that of the child becoming an adult, the seed becoming a vegetal or living being,

the acorn becoming an oak, and so on. Indeed, in *generation*, its experience and its empirical observation, one *sees* what was only seed or
origin develop and become plant, animal, or man, and one can follow
the process of engendering and growth in all its phases, *without any visible interruption.* The continuity of the process of engendering and development founds the continuity of the process of knowledge: one can
follow, in knowledge, *the very trace* of the process of genesis in reality
and reproduce it in the form of a genesis within thought.

To follow the very trace signifies something quite important: one
can follow the trace only of an *individual* that possesses an identity, that
is, an *identifiable* being that is always the same individual, that *always
possesses the same identity through all its transformations, its phases, or even
its mutations.* This amounts to saying that ultimately the thought of a
genesis tolerates quite well, despite what I have said, the ideal of mutations or even of discontinuities, on the *absolute condition* that one be
able to designate those mutations and discontinuities in the development of a previously *identified* selfsame individual that is thus identifiable as the constant support of those—or *its*—mutations and discontinuities. This is what allows all adepts of genesis to believe that they are
dialecticians, for it is enough for them to talk about stages or mutations
to believe that they have thus, and at minimal cost, purchased dialectical credentials (this is the case of Hegel and of all his disciples, even the
unwitting ones).

If, then, one can follow the trace only of an identified individual, it
is identifiable *from the inception*, otherwise the very project of "elaborating its genesis" disappears (I will return to that question in an instant, since it contains a relevant contradiction). This corresponds to
what is implied in the connotative system of the concept of genesis: in
every genesis the individual of the end (what is to be engendered) is
contained *in germ* from the *inception* of its process of engendering. The
oak is contained in the acorn; the oak is already entirely within the
acorn. As you know, in the seventeenth century Malebranche, who was
merely taking up the biological theories current at the time, saw that
theoretical necessity as taking the form of a theory of *preformation*:
within the tulip bulb is already, *entirely formed,* a small tulip (long live
the microscope!).[11] That theory of preformation served admirably the
dogma of original sin, but let us move on. Hegel accorded that exi-
gency latent in the concept of genesis its open and explicit form, its
conceptual form: the end is the beginning, which means that the be-

ginning (the *origin* in the strict sense, the *birth* of an identified individual) already contains, if not already formed (in itself and for itself), at least in germ, *in itself*, the term of the developmental process.

That implication, which may appear to be excessive in my crude presentation of it, no doubt haunts, without its "practitioners" realizing it, *every use* of the concept of genesis. One can express it still more compactly by saying that the structure of every genesis is necessarily teleological: if the end is already, in itself, in germ, virtually, etc., present from the beginning-origin, it is because every process is *governed by its end*, tends toward its end (a profoundly Aristotelian thought). Once again, this may appear to be rather "crude," but it possesses a very real sense in the practice of adepts of genesis; one detects it quite easily in the fact that they assign themselves the task of working out the genesis of a phenomenon that is always *identified in advance*, and it is the birth of that *already identified* individual that they want to *witness*, that they want to have us witness. Every genetic thought is literally obsessed by the search for a "birth," with all that is entailed by the ambiguity of that word, which presupposes, among other ideological temptations, the (most frequently implicit or misperceived) idea that what is to be observed in its very birth *already bears its name*, already possesses its identity, is thus to a certain extent already identifiable, already exists in some manner *before its own birth* in order to be born! It would be extremely interesting to see the source of the retrospective illusion that projects onto the *order* of the process of engendering in reality the very order of the process of knowledge. (Indeed, to know the "genesis" of phenomenon A, one must begin with the end, that is, with the existence and identification of said phenomenon A; *one always starts with the result* in knowledge, for it is there that the *order* of knowledge consists. The illusion consists in *extending* that order of the process of knowledge to the real process, at which point one imagines that in the actual process in reality the beginning contains the term in itself, that is, the identified individual whose birth one is supposed to be witnessing.) But this retrospective illusion, which takes the order of the process of knowledge for the order of the process in reality, is no doubt possible solely for purely ideological reasons, in whose details it is not possible to enter here, but one of whose effects can be grasped quite vividly in the ceremonies occurring around the simple birth of a child: he bears a name before being born, and if by chance he has not yet been assigned one, one at least knows that *it is a child* that is about to be born. Let us say things squarely: when one wants to think through the "genesis" of the unconscious, one starts with the result, one starts with the result within knowledge, namely, the existence of that identified "individual" called the unconscious, and elaborating the genesis of the unconscious consists in moving back to its birth, to the point at which one witnesses its birth, but one manages only with difficulty to rid oneself of the idea that in a certain way, to elaborate the genesis of the unconscious means to seek out, even before its birth, all that already *prefigures and announces* it, already contains it in person, even in the form of a draft, but that resembles it and *that is already it*, that already bears its name, that is already *identifiable*, if not as the unconscious, at least as what will be, and that is thus already more or less in itself the unconscious. One has the greatest difficulty conceiving that prior to the unconscious absolutely *nothing* exists that resembles the unconscious; one always tends to recognize it in germ, as a promise, draft, element, prefiguration, etc., *before its own birth* precisely because one conceives its *irruption* in the form of a *birth*. One can grasp the same fault beneath each of the concepts connoting the meaning of the concept of genesis, but the concept of birth (origin) allows one to see it in all clarity, despite the profound resistances against the critique of the concept of *birth*. (You have surely many things to say on those resistances. I am thinking in particular of the fantasy according to which each person has a hard time imagining that he did not exist *prior to* his own birth, in other words, that he has not for all eternity been endowed with the *right* to be born, the right to his own existence, to his own birth; the terror of the counterfantasy—"and what if it weren't I who was born?" or "what would become of *me* if I hadn't been born, but if another had been *born in my place?*"—bears sufficient witness to this.)

I have already said enough on the subject (and no doubt a good deal too much!) at least to suggest what follows. Like every ideological concept, the concept of genesis recognizes while *misconstruing*, that is, it *designates* a reality even as it covers it over with a false knowledge, an illusion. The illusion-misconstruing of the concept of genesis (and of its *current* connotations: this is a semantico-theoretical state of things, which we can change only by acknowledging its existence and effects) consists fundamentally in proposing that we think the *irruption* of a new reality (phenomenon A) subordinate to the *obligatory* concept of birth as it offers itself and indeed is, that is, charged with ideological connotations that it owes to its place of origin, or rather, to its *field of use* (that of human birth, birth par excellence, of which other forms of birth—animal, vegetable, etc.—are but subexamples). Through that *obligatory* confusion (the ideology of genesis doesn't leave us a choice: it *obliges* us to think every irruption *as a birth*), however, through that misconstruction, the concept of genesis does indeed *designate* a *reality* that can be thought only on the condition of rejecting the concepts of its miscognition. That reality is (I adopt your term, which seems to me, *in the current state* of things, that is, of concepts, *the best*) the *irruption* of phenomenon A, which is radically new in relation to all that has preceded its own irruption.

Whence the imperative of a *logic* different from that of *genesis*, but precisely to *think* that reality and not to *dispense* with thinking that reality. I have for a long time now been insisting on the necessity of constituting that new logic, which amounts to the same thing as defining the specific forms of a materialist dialectic. And yet, in indicating that necessity I have barely uttered anything more than critical propositions or analyzed forms belonging to the theory of history. One must go further, but I have not yet broached that "further."

To advance "further," allow me to step back for an instant and focus on a contradiction that every geneticist ambition bears within itself and resolves only through recourse to the concepts of miscognition about which I have spoken (origin, birth, etc.). That contradiction, which geneticist ideology does not assume, which it refuses to confront, which it avoids broaching and thinking, with which it resorts to ruses, before which it would escape, is the following: ultimately, "to undertake the genesis" of a phenomenon means to explain how it was born *from what is not it*. To undertake the genesis of A is to explain through what mechanism not-A (what is *other than* A) produces A. To assume or take on that contradiction is to accept that what one is seeking in order to explain the mechanism through which A irrupts *is not* A, nor is it its prefiguration, germ, draft, promise, etc. (all expressions that are but *tendentious* metaphors, by which I mean metaphors *tending* to enforce the belief that A can be born only from A, just as a *little man* is born of a *man*); it is at the same time to accept that the mechanism through which A irrupts from other than A is not the mechanism of engendering or the development of the germ or seed. The two imperatives are linked: if A is not born of A, the mechanism through which A irrupts from non-A cannot be the *mechanism* through which, in the ideological figure of genesis, A is born from A, the mechanism of engendering and development or, to refer to still more primitive ideological figures, the mechanism of genesis in the biblical sense in which the *thought* precedes the thing created, the thing produced, in which the idea, the project, the (desired) order, is the logical "seed" (in the spermatic sense of the Logos of John and the Stoics) of the reality, *the thing itself preceding its own birth*. (That's why I said that at bottom every thought of genesis is religious.)

You see that I by no means refuse the problem of *explaining* the *irruption* of a phenomenon A, but at least in the case that concerns us (since the effects of the precedence of an individual in relation to its own birth that I invoked with relation to the geneticist ideology deserve attention, even if they are the site of an illusion, whether it be the man who precedes the man in procreation or "the plan preceding the house in the architect's head," as Marx puts it in a sentence in *Capital*, in which some have taken idealist delight), that explanation is possible only *on two conditions*:

(a) renouncing the search for whatever, before the "birth" of A, "resembles" (germ, prefiguration, draft, promise, presentiment, etc.) A but searching instead for what effectively *intervenes* in the production of the "A effect" (in this case, the unconscious) and that in all likelihood does not "resemble" A (neither the machine tool that presses it, nor the metal, nor the work expended, nor the electricity and other elements that intervene in the production of a pot "resemble"—or are the "seed," the draft, etc., of—the said pot);

(b) searching for the *specific mechanism* that produces the irruption of the "A effect," beginning by giving up the belief that this mechanism can have something in common with the mechanisms induced by the ideology of genesis, namely, the mechanisms of procreation, development, *filiation*, etc.

I would willingly add to those two conditions a third: whereas the ideology of genesis presupposes that one can "follow the trace" of birth, and as a result it considers only what *resembles* the effect to be explained, thus only what is most similar to it and the most *visibly close*, this new logic can provoke the *intervention* of elements that at first sight do not seem to be directly in question and may even seem to be *absent* from the conditions of phenomenon A. I believe you will agree with the very general principle that *absence* possesses a certain efficacy on the condition, to be sure, that it be not absence in general, nothingness, or any other Heideggerian "openness" but a *determinate* absence playing a role in the space of its absence. This is undoubtedly important for the problem of the irruption of the unconscious.

Concerning that "new" logic, I would have things to say, but they are as yet too precarious to be uttered *in general*, precisely under the form of a logic, or more precisely a dialectic (what I specified in the essay "On the Materialist Dialectic" in *For Marx* is merely the study of *certain effects* and concerns only indirectly the problem of a logic of irruption). I prefer to take *one* example on which we have worked.

It concerns the problem of the irruption mechanism of *one* determined mode of production, the capitalist mode of production. When one reads *Capital* rather closely, it appears that contrary to the genetic ideology currently applied to Marx (or the evolutionist ideology, which is the same thing), the capitalist mode of production was not "engendered" by the feudal mode of production as its own *son*. There is no *filiation* properly (precisely) speaking between the feudal mode of production and the capitalist mode of production. The capitalist mode of production irrupts from the *encounter* (another one of your concepts to which I subscribe entirely) of a certain number of very precise elements and from the specific *combination* of those *elements* ("combination" translates the Marxist concept of *Verbindung*: your concept of *organization* would fit quite well, or the concept of *arrangement*). The feudal mode of production *engenders* (as a father engenders his son, among other productions—his children constituting only part of his Complete Works, whether written or not) only those *elements*, of which certain ones, moreover (the accumulation of money in the form of capital), go back to before the feudal mode of production or can be produced by other modes of production. The feudal mode of production in no way *engenders* either the *encounter* of those elements or the fact that they can *combine and organize themselves* in an actual unit that *functions*, an actual functioning unit that is precisely *what irrupts*. The fact that those elements are elements apt to combine (not all things eager to combine can!), the fact that they begin to function as a mode of production, and the fact that their functioning represents a real mode of production—*all that is absolutely without any genetic relation with the feudal mode of production* but obeys instead laws entirely different from those of engendering by the feudal mode of production, laws one could never find in observing the effects of the feudal mode of production, in particular turning over as many times as one wants those *elements* that were, however, in fact engendered by the feudal mode of production. To attain those laws (which are, in fact, the laws of combination in general, a combination that is always *specific*, constitutive of every mode of production) one must renounce looking for them in the immediate proximity of phenomenon A or in anything that "resembles" it in the conditions of its "birth." They are not *visible* in that proximity, since phenomena close or similar to A concern only the nature of those elements, on the one hand, and the mechanisms of the feudal mode of production alone, on the other. The observation of those sole close or similar phenomena does not contribute anything; one must observe *other* phenomena that are *pertinent* to what occurs in the encounter and combination of the elements producing A and not the phenomena that are pertinent *only* to what constitutes those elements.

(To fix our ideas, I will indicate very crudely which are the *elements* indispensable to their combination functioning in reality as a new mode of production: the capitalist mode of production. Those elements are above all: (1) the existence of money accumulated in the form of capital; (2) the existence of a great mass of "workers" who have become "free"—that is, stripped of their means of production; (3) a certain threshold crossed in the development of techniques for the transformation of nature—energetic, mechanical, chemical, and biological techniques—and techniques for the organization of labor (division, cooperation). History shows several situations in which only two of those elements are united, but not the third; in such cases no new mode of production irrupts, and the capitalist mode of production is not "born.")

We find in that example the two essential points that preoccupy you. For Marx does indeed propose to explain the mode of *irruption* of a new reality, but he can do it, despite several formulations of a Hegelian or evolutionist stamp, only by rejecting, in the practice of his theoretical work, the concepts of genesis (the Hegelian concepts); he thus does indeed propose to resolve a problem that you call (and that we can call provisionally for heuristic reasons) *diachronic*. And at the same time, once the *new* structure has *irrupted*, it functions *atemporally, exactly like* the unconscious. Marx says precisely that every mode of production is "eternal," which is a bit much coming from a man who spent his time explaining that the capitalist mode of production was historically conditioned and thus limited, perishable, and mortal!

When he says that the mode of production is "eternal," he means that it functions in a closed circuit, in the mode of atemporality, and that far from being subject to the temporality of "chronology," that is, of temporal succession, or of historicity in the common sense, it is independent of it; *exactly like* the unconscious, it *reproduces itself* endlessly, and that atemporal "synchronic" reproduction is the absolute condition of its "production" in the economic sense as in all other senses. He means by this that the forms of historical temporality observable in the "historical period" of the capitalist mode of production are determined as historical and as the forms they are by the atemporal, eternal structure of the said mode of production.

The "eternity" of the mode of production is no more incompatible with the actual *history*, the determined historical temporality that is produced under the mode of production in question, than the *actual history* of the individual is incompatible with the atemporality of the unconscious. In both cases that actual history is determined by the ahistory of the structure (in one case the mode of production, in the other the unconscious).

But all these distinctions and their efforts at clarification are possible only on the condition that one sees well that neither the *temporality* of the irruption of a new structure nor the *temporality* of its functioning (mode of production or unconscious) is reducible to what is commonly called time or simple chronology and its apparent exigencies. The "allure" of the concrete temporality of so-called chronological history, which can be "observed" in either the irruption ("birth") of a new structure or in its functioning, is always unintelligible in and by itself; it can be understood only as the *effect* of the functioning of a mechanism, be it the mechanism of the irruption or that of the functioning of the structure. The meaning to be attributed to simple chronology (and I agree that it should not be neglected, that it imposes a before and an after, but it does not go any further and, on the other hand, risks a certain confusion by inspiring a search, as in every linear, nonstructural causality, for the reason for the immediate "after" in the immediate "before," in the visible "before") is itself determined by the structure of that temporality, a structure determined in the last instance by the structural mechanisms at play—whether they be of the irruption or the functioning of some new structure: a new mode of production, the unconscious, etc.

I don't know whether I have been clear and whether I haven't, in the desire to illuminate certain points, obscured or completely lost sight of other important points. But for the moment I can barely go any further. What I am telling you here summarizes a certain number of things that I would like to set forth in a future essay. You will thus be my first witness (I should make clear that a number of these things have already been expressed by Balibar in his text in *Reading "Capital," II*).

(2) I now broach other points about which, as you will soon be convinced, I am infinitely less well informed . . .

First the thesis: "the unconscious is structured like a language."

I fear that there is a misunderstanding between us. Look at what you say at the beginning of your letter. I don't believe we are talking about the same thing. You in fact look for a meaning for this thesis by saying that "the conscious-preconscious/unconscious relation is on the order of the signified/signifier relation." This means, if I understand you well, (1) that language is indeed an "essential element of the preconscious" (or of the conscious), but not of the unconscious, (2) that the linguistic relation that you retain as pertinent in this case is the signifier/signified relation, and (3) that it is played out between the unconscious (signifier?) and the preconscious-conscious (signified?).

But in the preceding thesis it is a matter not of the conscious and the preconscious but solely of the *unconscious*. Moreover, it is not said that the unconscious is language or a language, or that language plays a role in it, occupies an essential or secondary place in it; it is said that the unconscious is *structured like* a language. This means first of all that it is not language, a language, etc. (and in particular that the question of knowing whether language in the strict sense plays a role in it is an entirely different question), and then that what makes it resemble ("like") a language is its "structure."

It is thus a matter of a *resemblance of structure* between the unconscious and language; the thesis says nothing else. It in no way says that the unconscious is a language or is reducible to a language, etc. It in no way says, among other things, that the elements structured in the unconscious are identical or comparable to the elements that are structured in language. In other words, there can be no question of reducing the theory of the unconscious to a chapter or a subchapter of general linguistics . . .

A word now about that *structure*. It is not at all a question of the "signified/signifier relation." It cannot be said, it seems to me, that this "relation" is a "structure"; at least, Lacan is *absolutely not* speaking or think-ing about this when he utters his thesis. It seems to me that the "signi-fied/signifier relation" is an effect of signification, an effect that depends on the *structure* of language, said structure implementing *signi-fiers* (and not the signified/signifier relation). I think it is not quite by chance that you put that "relation" forward as identical to the structure of language, which is what is at stake in the thesis, and that you say that this relation can be observed *between* the conscious-preconscious, on the one hand (the signified?), and the unconscious, on the other (the signifier?). If the "structure of language" is that relation, *two* terms are needed, namely, the unconscious *plus* another term (the conscious-preconscious). If that relation is but a secondary structural effect of the *structure* of language (which concerns *only signifiers*), however, then one no longer needs a second term, and the thesis is perhaps false, but at least it is coherent: the unconscious can be structured like a language without needing (as in your hypothesis) a second term (which is not the unconscious!) in order to exist in its structure. On this point Lacan is quite logical in his own terms: he says not that the "unconscious *and* the conscious-preconscious are structured like . . ." but that the *uncon-scious* (alone) is structured like a language, and the structure he speaks about is such that it indeed has no need of a second term. In point of fact, you will not find that for him the *structure* of the unconscious con-cerns "the signified/signifier relation" (since that "relation" is but one of its "effects"); he speaks not of that relation but constantly of the *mechanisms of combination of the signifiers*. The "laws" of those mecha-nisms are what constitute the "structure" at stake in the thesis, that structure *through* which the unconscious resembles (and solely by virtue of it) language.

If such be the case, I do not see wherein Freud's great contribution ("the inseparability of the triple—topographical, dynamic, and eco-nomic—point of view") would be threatened in principle by the the-sis in question. *It would be,* to be sure, if the "structure" in question were identified, as you identify it, with the "signified/signifier relation" (and it seems to me that one can interpret the first two of Freud's concep-tions—remembrance of the forgotten memory, then restitution of the repressed wish—as able to fall within a relation of the signified/signi-fier type, and at bottom, it was in that sense alone that Politzer under-stood Freud!). But the "structure" of language absolutely cannot be reduced to that "relation," even in the case of Saussure, for whom it is much more a *nonrelation* than a relation (cf. the theory of the *arbitrary* nature of the sign). To speak of a "relation" (but I have no wish to quarrel over words; I refer to an objective temptation) is to pull Saussure backward toward a linguistic theory of the eighteenth-century sort (where the central question is indeed that of the relation of signifier and signified, of the sign attached to the representation, on the one hand, and to the thing or object or idea, on the other).

To summarize my point, I believe that in the content you give to the thesis "the unconscious . . ." there is a double misunderstanding. *First of all*, there is a misunderstanding about the object in question: it is a matter solely of the unconscious and not of its relation to the conscious and the preconscious; the misunderstanding is compounded by an error involving the word "like" (which excludes the possibility that the unconscious might be *reduced* to language). *Then*, there is a misunderstanding concerning the meaning that the word *structure* might have in the expression "the unconscious is structured like. . . ." The "structure" alluded to is not the "signified/signifier relation" but the laws of combination governing the mechanisms of signifiers (what Freud *rediscovers* in displacement, condensation, etc.).

I do not claim to be able to give a satisfactory account of the questions *posed in that manner*; I wanted only to indicate *how* it seems to me that the questions should be posed, in what terms, in order to avoid the confusions I mentioned.

(3) A few words now on the second thesis: "the child is caught up in language from the time of his birth."

You are entirely correct: one can make a properly *metaphysical* use of this thesis, and if that is *the sole use* one can make of it, the thesis should be relegated to the storage bin of metaphysical contraptions and notorious mystifications, alongside ancestral memory, the collective unconscious, etc.

Nonetheless I am not entirely convinced by your demonstration. To put it differently, I do not think that you have proven that the sole use that can be made of that thesis is metaphysical. I am going to attempt to tell you why, but there too I am on extremely fragile ground (for me).

I believe that your demonstration is possible only on the condition that one considerably restricts the meaning of the expression "caught in language," and more particularly the meaning of "language." I am, moreover, considerably guilty of that reduction-restriction, since I have not at all specified in what sense the word *language* was to be understood.

If I take up your formulas, I believe I can observe that you take the word *language* in the sense that is, *crudely speaking*, designated by post-Saussurean linguists when they talk of "speech" [*parole*]. I do not think I am forcing your thought, or deforming it. On the reverse side of page 3, you make use of the following formula: "*communication* through language necessitates confrontation . . ." And that formula seems to me to designate precisely all the examples you take, whether it be a matter of the perception or nonperception of meaning, of utterance, of its anticipation, etc. Now "communication through language" designates rather well what linguists call "speech" [parole], that is, to use an expression I would risk, one of the *concrete forms* or *modalities of existence* of *language*. Language [*la. langue*] is the *structure* (which is "two-tiered": a system of phonemes and their regulated combinations and a system of morphemes and their regulated combinations) that constitutes the *condition of possibility* of all its concrete forms or modalities of existence, among which figures *speech* [*la parole*] (the concrete form of existence in which the "function" of *communication* you discuss is "exercised"). "Speech" is not language [*la langue*] but one of its concrete forms or modalities of existence.

If one were to *reduce* the phrase "the child is caught up in language [*le langage*]" to this other phrase, "the child is caught up in speech" or "communication," I grant you entirely that one would be vulnerable to a metaphysical use of the phrase, and you would be entirely right to retort to me that during a whole period the child is not, *cannot be*, caught up "in speech," since it has no "meaning" for him, it doesn't *exist* for him as "speech," since the defining characteristic of all "speech" is to be perceived and understood as meaningful and to call for a "response"—*parole*, then, presupposes the existence of a speaker and a listener and of a listener-speaker. All your examples are indeed related to that question, and the problem you have posed is indeed the problem of the *irruption in the child* of the listener-speaker or, if you prefer, of the behavior of speech. It is a *real problem*, but it is not the problem I was (awkwardly) intent on indicating. In point of fact, I wanted to indicate a problem *prior* in principle (and also in fact) to this problem of the irruption of speech behavior, which is a *derivative* problem.

The first problem that I wanted to indicate concerns not speech but language [*la langue*]. If such be the case, the terms of the problem change, and the meaning of the problem changes too. To express things quite crudely, I will go so far as to say that the formula "the child is caught up from the time of his birth *in language* [*la langue*]" (to the extent that *la langue* is an abstract structure, the condition of possibility of its concrete forms of existence) must be interpreted *in a very broad sense*, which is to be found, it seems to me (unless I am misconstruing his thought) in Lacan: "the child is caught up from the time of his birth *in the symbolic*," of which language [*la langue*] constitutes the *formal system*. What is *the symbolic?* Here I shall venture forth at my own risk. The symbolic order is an order subject to laws. What makes it, in relation to what interests us here, a *symbolic* order is that it is an order (or a structure) that always includes (in all its "levels") *two stories or tiers* exactly as language [*la langue*] contains a phonological story and the story of signifiers, which exist as signifiers (*units of meaning*) only on the condition of existing *simultaneously* as composed of *units of sound*. That *double articulation* constitutes the essence of the *symbolic* order insofar as it is symbolic, and what constitutes the specificity of the symbolic is that the first articulation (the "first story") is determined by the second (the "second story"). That last observation means that, in the example of language [*la langue*], since I have taken that example, it is the division into *units of meaning* (morphemes, which are themselves minimal signifiers) that allows us to determine the *division into units of sound*. The specificity of the symbolic is thus that its "first story," without which the "second" would not exist (there are no signifiers without sounds), is *determined* in its "divisions" and in its laws by the "second story," which allows, within the first story, a whole "play" of the phonematic elements that, among other things, *create the possibility of* slips of the tongue, the garbling of words, puns, etc. I am indicating only a general principle here.

If I come back now, after this detour, to the thesis that the child "is caught up from the time of his birth in language," which should be understood as "in the Symbolic," I believe that one can grant a meaning to that thesis, a meaning that is not metaphysical. What it means is that the child irrupts as a biological being *within* the system of the *symbolic order*. He is caught up in it from his birth exactly as he is caught "from birth" *within* the element of the atmosphere. He is cast into the one at the same time as into the other. His exchanges with the atmosphere are regulated biologically. His exchanges with the "symbolic medium" (which is perfectly objective) into which he is also cast are regulated in an entirely different manner.

We thus hold the two ends of the chain. The child is born as a small animal cast into a world that is structured by the symbolic order and its regions. That is the first link. That order becomes *his* order, that is, he occupies *his* place in it (in the strong sense of *his*, for it has become *his* in the process) on emerging from the Oedipus complex. That is the last link. When he leaves that transition, transformation, or adventure, we observe that he possesses *an unconscious* and that the unconscious is part of the conditions (it is not the only one!) indispensable for the child to "function" as a little "human" child, that is, an inhabitant, a "full" citizen (even if she be "little") of that symbolic order, that human world (which is the same).

I agree with you that it is imperative to account for the *irruption* of that "part" indispensable to the "functioning" of the "human" psyche, that is, a psyche functioning as a "subject" of a human—that is, symbolic—world. We agree that, to account for the irruption of the unconscious, one *has to start from the result*, namely, the indispensable existence of the unconscious and all the properties that can be attributed to it as *essential*, properties that may be detected through an experience and a practice of the unconscious in analytic therapy (the privileged site for an experience of the unconscious). That certain of those properties appear to be of the first importance and that among them some can serve as indirect *indices* of what could have produced the irruption of the unconscious are also certain, but we do not know *in advance* which of the characteristics of the unconscious that we may discover in it in analytic therapy can offer the *indices*, can serve as indices for raising the question of the irruption of the unconscious. We are obliged to start out in search of those pertinent characteristics, taking into account the exhaustive array not only of characteristics (and of the functioning) of the unconscious that we manage to know through analytic practice but also and *at the same time* of the elements that are *present at the other end of the chain.* It is through an unending oscillation from one end to the other of the chain that we can hope to cast some light on the mechanism of the process that produced the irruption of the unconscious.

It is at this juncture that the *bringing together* of the two theses I indicated to you can take on meaning: "the unconscious is structured like a language," and the child is "caught up from birth in language" (or the symbolic).

Let's look at the two theses a bit more closely, now that we may suspect that their articulation may have a relation with our problem (knowledge of the mechanism producing the irruption of the unconscious).

(a) That the unconscious is structured *like* a language stems from the analysis of the *results* acquired by analytic practice.

This does not mean that the unconscious *is* language [*la langue*]. It means that its structure resembles ("like") that of a "language" [*le langage*]. It means, in the broader sense, that its structure resembles that of the symbolic, *with two tiers or stories*. If I am not wrong, the two stories are in Freud, as is the link with "language" [*le langage*]. I might risk saying that the elements of the first story are constituted by fragments of the *imaginary*, divided into primary units and possessing laws of arrangement, but that those primary units are not signifiers of the unconscious: they constitute only the "body" of unconscious signifiers (like the units of *sound* or phonemes constituting the "body" of linguistic signifiers), which obey other laws of combination and arrangement. I don't dare go very much further (my ignorance), but those other laws of combination, arranging other units (the unconscious signifiers, which can certainly be words, but *also something entirely different*), seem subject, in their formal aspect, to the linguistic laws of displacement and condensation, which are similar to ("like") the laws of metonymy and metaphor. The units on which they bear are in no way the units of meaning of verbal language, and all the more emphatically the elements (the first story) that constitute them are in no way *sounds*, but *formally*, the unconscious possesses a structure related to that of language [*la langue*], without the unconscious for all that being language [*la langue*] or a language [*une langue*]. Would you subscribe to such formulations? They leave completely open the question of the *specific nature* of the units constitutive of the first story (fragments of the imaginary, "pieces" of the unconscious), as well as the specific nature of the units of the second story (signifiers of the unconscious); they even go a lot further *by ruling out* that the nature of those units might be the same as that of the corresponding units of *language* [*la langue*].

That is what can be retained at this end of the chain. Now let's travel to the *other end of the chain*.

(b) "The child is caught up from birth *in* language."

If one gives that sentence the broad meaning I indicated, in which language [*le langage*] = symbolic order, it may be said that indeed the child is cast and falls *into* that order on being born. *That he does not perceive it* does not play any role: neither the child nor even men in general perceive the layer of air beneath which they live, either. The question is not one of knowing whether the child perceives in order to decide that the order exists: he is subject to it. He will "perceive" it only once he is inscribed within it, in his place (after the Oedipus complex), "full-fledged"; he will have become not merely a speaker but a manipulator on his own of categories other than those of spoken language, for instance, categories of kinship (father, mother, child, little sister, etc.).

If we want to proceed without adding anything to the *facts*, there too, when we wonder what happens when the child "falls" into life, we ought to take a precise inventory of the *elements*, the *characteristics* constituting the milieu into which he is "thrown." And we should make that inventory without recourse to principles too far removed, or to imaginary principles, but without neglecting the *nature* of the elements effectively present in that milieu and constituting it.

In that immediate familial milieu (for that is what constitutes what the child "falls" into, and not society in general or "culture" in general), we can count the following:

1. the part of that region of the symbolic constituted by familial structures (kinship structures as they exist at the child's birth): the current monogamous couple, with all the (positive or negative) rules of relation;

2. the concerned parts of that *other* region of the symbolic constituted by the *existing ideological forms* in which the kinship structures considered are concretely lived (the ideological form of the couple, the father, the mother, paternity, and maternity and the ideological, moral, and religious forms attached to those parental ideological forms) (the parental ideological forms being *dominated* in our societies by those moral, juridical, and religious ideological forms) (with all their positive-negative relations); and

3. that other very particular "region" of the symbolic which is *language* [*la langue*], which functions, as I have tried to show, as the form of circulation of the other regions' elements among themselves.

It is in and under those structures of the symbolic regions under consideration that the concrete characters populating the "family milieu" into which the child is "thrown" *exist*. Those characters thus function as full-fledged members of that symbolic universe (the family milieu), which is itself open (or closed, it is all the same) to the other symbolic spaces of social reality. As subjects of the symbolic, they are endowed with an unconscious (that is, one of its possible "malformations"), but they also possess other *pieces* in their mechanism to be able to function as subjects of the symbolic (instances other than the unconscious and the "faculties" attached to them, perception-consciousness, "moral conscience," speaker-listener behavior, etc.). The *reality* of the regions of the symbolic and of the structure of the symbolic as such is "realized" in those characters who simultaneously inhabit and constitute the family milieu into which the child "falls." Saying that the child lives under the law of *his* parents, under the law of the rules "realized" by their concrete behavior (gestures, attitudes, attention, distractions, etc., including that maternal anticipation of which you do well to speak), is one and the same thing as saying that he lives under the law of the regional *structures* of the symbolic that *exist* in the form of his parents.

To say that his parents are subjects of the symbolic does not mean that they are *formal* beings. If they have an unconscious, it means in particular that their "biological" existence is realized in the form of *unconscious* wishes and that the unconscious is one of the specific structures under which they live their "biological" existence under the law of the symbolic. For them, the problem that the child will have to resolve *is already resolved*, and their already achieved solution is part of the given elements of the problem the child is going to have to solve.

To say that the child lives under the law of the unconscious of his parents or under the law of the kinship structure binding them, of the structure of the ideology in which they live their relations to their conditions, [or] to say that the child lives under the law of the symbolic *is to say one and the same thing*. To say that the child is caught from birth in language is to say exactly this, if you are willing to grant that extension (language = structure of the regions of the symbolic involved in the constitution of the child's "milieu") to the term *language* [*le langage*]. It is also to say that he lives under the law of *language* [*la langue*], even though he is no doubt sensitive to the effects of spoken language only after a certain threshold of neurological and motor "maturation" (you are undoubtedly right to recall it) has been reached; he is nonetheless subject (*even if it be to escape it*) from the beginning to that universe, which is definable only by its essence, which is *symbolic*.

The *articulation* of these two theses (each firmly established on its own), that the unconscious is "structured like a language" and that the child is "caught from birth under the law of the symbolic" (in the specific forms conferred on it by the reality of the family milieu), *seems to make evident* something in common: namely, the structures of the symbolic in general. Whence (Lacan's) hypothesis that the structures of language (say, of the symbolic) play a determining role in the mechanisms issuing in the irruption of the unconscious. Whence, however, the imperative of having to account for the specificity of the specific *substructure* that is the unconscious, produced by the effect of the structures of the symbolic.

Such would thus be the global and, to be sure, *provisional* result of this first oscillation between the results obtained at the two ends of the chain: to search for the components of the mechanism producing the irruption of the unconscious among the *structures* of the symbolic while taking into account the fact that the elements of which they are the structures are *specific* to the very particular structure that is the unconscious (these elements are those fragments of the imaginary rediscovered in the analysis of the unconscious, or rather of its *formations*, which are its modes of concrete existence).

All this is not at all incompatible with what you say about the observation of the child, which no doubt concerns one of the *moments* of the *manifestation* of one of the essential conditions for the structuration of the unconscious: the binary absence-presence relation of the mother with the child and the elaboration of the first forms of *speech*. But what occurs in this directly observable phenomenon and seems to be the *origin* of the unconscious is but a *datable effect* of the effectiveness of the entire system of elements that were put in place from birth and that play in extremely complex and diverse forms (the rhythms of the mother's presence, sphincter training, etc.), without it being possible to assign a punctual, radical *origin* from which a *filiation* might be thought, at the "birth" of the unconscious. The unconscious irrupts not as the effect of a series of linear causes but as the effect of a complex causality, which may be termed *structural* (without center, without origin), made of the *idiosyncratic combination* of the structural forms presiding over the "birth" (the irruption) of the unconscious. A meaning can be assigned to observations of the pathology of language in the context of this structural causality: if this or that observable manifestation is indeed a datable effect—itself a moment of the constitution of the unconscious—of the "structural causality" presiding over the production of the new structure that is the unconscious, since it is only a *partial* and derivative *effect of it* and since it is not primal, it can inflect the development of the child in one direction or another; there is a "play" of variations possible (from the normal to the slightly and then the seriously pathological) in the existence of that effect. This would not be the case if the effect were the effect of a filiation, an identifiable and assignable cause; in that case it would not allow for any "play." It includes "play" solely because it is a structural effect whose meaning will appear only later, according to the place assumed by the effect in the emerging structure, or rather in the structure once constituted. It would be interesting to examine the following point: *starting at* what degree of complexity, what type of arrangement of observable effects, can one infer with certainty that a specific evolution will occur? Child pathology must be rich in observations allowing this question to be raised and, in certain cases, to be answered. I mean that certain effects must be "left hanging," *not yet* having received their definitive meaning, [not yet] authorizing a diagnosis, whereas others must already be quite indicatory, allowing for a diagnosis. It would be interesting to study the *differences* existing in the nature of these effects that do or do not permit a diagnosis. You will see that far from excluding observation, the position I am indicating, on the contrary, demands it, but it simultaneously allows one to determine the kind of pertinent question that may be addressed to the observed data. The position I am proposing is not a priori since it rests on *facts* (those of the two ends of the chain): it can be validated only by its confrontation with intermediate observations, of which those you cite are without any doubt the most important, but the *meaning* of those intermediate observations can be truly ascertained only through confrontation with the conclusions drawn from other facts (which are also describable as results of observation, be they results of analytic practice or of the inventory of structural elements presiding over the existence of the child cast into the family world). Only this new oscillation can allow one to verify a hypothesis concerning the productive mechanism governing the irruption of the unconscious or to assign their authentic meaning to intermediate observations.

You will perhaps say that I am rather far from Lacan in maintaining this discourse. Perhaps, since I don't know him, but it matters little after all, and in any event it was what I was able to perceive of him that put me on this path. There can't be smoke without fire. But let's leave this point to come to a final hypothesis, which is perhaps more risky that all the others but to which I am bound, around which I have been "turning" for quite a bit of time, and whose first judge you shall also be.

I will undoubtedly distance myself from Lacan (even though it's not absolutely sure) by risking the formulation of another connection between what can be observed at the two ends of the chain.

We agree that once it is constituted, the unconscious functions as an "atemporal" structure. I will use a comparison here: once it has been *set up*, and set up to be able to function, an *engine* always "functions" with *something*. For example, a gas engine functions with gasoline. Now I wonder whether one can't say that the unconscious also needs "something" to function, and this "something" is, it seems to me, in the last analysis, *the stuff of ideology*. On this point I would have to sketch an explanation of what the ideological is. It is enough for our present purpose to know that the ideological cannot be reduced to the conceptual systems of ideology but is an *imaginary* structure that exists not only in the form of concepts but also in the form of attitudes, gestures, patterns of behavior, intentions, aspirations, refusals, permissions, bans, etc. Moreover, can't one say that the forms of manifestation of the unconscious, which obey *repetition*, are repeated only in defined conditions whose *realization*—or "setup"—is ensured by the unconscious, but on the condition of "finding" in situations that are "experienced" (that "experience" which is precisely ideology in action, the realization of a *specific* ideological form) the wherewithal for ensuring that "setup"? The unconscious can exploit anything to its ends, but it still has to "find" something suitable to its ends. To say that the unconscious "functions with ideological imaginary" is thus to say that it "selects" in the ideological imaginary the forms, elements, or relations "suitable" to it. I have the impression that it is not by chance that certain ideological "situations" sustain certain defined unconscious structures marvelously well and that "affinities" exist between a specific form of neurosis, and even psychosis, with the result that a particular conjuncture "realizes" par excellence specific unconscious structures. One could see this during the wars (the "decline" in mental illness) and more particularly in certain political regimes whose ideologies "authorized" and "fueled" the "play" of a whole series of unconscious "re-actions." One would thus have to "read," *against the grain* of the meaning all too often proposed, the "unleashing" of "instincts" under Nazi, racist ideology as a general and official (and thus public and permissive) distribution of that ideological "fuel" needed by certain perversions to "function" in the *open* air. What can thus be seen in crude terms in situations as manifest as this can be discerned as well in more "private" situations, in which there is no longer, at least in its general form and as a form of public generosity, any "distribution" of ideological fuel for the functioning of psychotic, neurotic, or perverse structures; in such cases each unconscious is reduced to its own devices to procure its "drug," that is, the ideological "fuel" with which it works, the kind of "experience" (what is "experienced" is always shot through with ideology) in which it can be "realized." Does what I am advancing make sense? Does it correspond, even at a distance, to your analytic experience? My language will perhaps offend you. I can make use of a different—and perhaps less metaphorical—one. Might one not say, for instance, that every unconscious structure always tends to "lodge" in preexisting ideological forms, such as those in which it "functions" in conditions that satisfy it?

If such be the case, and if I *link* this imperative of the unconscious, which demands definite forms of ideology to be able to "function," with what it is possible to observe at the other end of the chain, namely, the presence among the regional structures of the symbolic presiding over the mechanism that produces the "irruption" of the unconscious [. . . ,][12] I would be tempted, *as a hypothesis*, to wonder whether the ideological forms in which the roles of characters of the family milieu are experienced do not have a *determining* influence on the structuration of the unconscious. I would not want to go too far or too quickly down this risky path, but it seems to me that there are deep affinities between the *nature* of elements of the ideological imaginary and the nature of elements of the unconscious imaginary, on the one hand, and between the mechanisms governing their combination on the "second story" of their respective structures [on the other hand]. This would lead me to consider that one would have to go a bit further than the thesis that the unconscious is structured like a language and say that the unconscious is structured like that "language [*langage*]" (which is not a *langue*) which is the *ideological* and that this resemblance of structures must be understood in a far more elaborate sense than in

the case of the "resemblance" between the structure of the unconscious and that of language. It would be a matter of a resemblance that
would no longer be merely *formal* but would call into play affinities of
matter (the imaginary) and of organizational structure (thus at a degree further toward the concrete). To be sure, it is not a matter of rein-
stating a new genesis-filiation; the structure of the unconscious is a
structure *other* than that of the ideological.

3

The Tbilisi Affair

1976–1984

INVITED BY LÉON CHERTOK—*with whom he had maintained good relations for a number of years*[1]—*to participate in the International Symposium on the Unconscious organized from October 1 to 5, 1979, at Tbilisi by the Academy of Sciences of Georgia and the University of Tbilisi in collaboration with the Déjerine Center for Psychosomatic Medicine in Paris (directed by Léon Chertok, who was vice-president of the colloquium), Louis Althusser wrote in the spring of 1976 a presentation entitled "The Discovery of Dr. Freud." In addition to sending a copy to Chertok, Althusser sent this first typed text of twenty-two pages to several of his intimates, notably Elisabeth Roudinesco, Fernand Deligny, Jacques Nassif, and Michel Pêcheux, asking them to communicate to him without any restraint their criticism of what he himself considered to be, as he wrote to Elisabeth Roudinesco on June 30, 1976, a "first draft," a "(hasty, perfunctory) project.*" On the same day he wrote in identical terms to Jacques Nassif: "*Here is the basic text [. . .] written, then, in great haste. Skip over the nonsense and give me your* detailed opinion *in writing as to what is fine, what isn't, what is lacking, false, falsified, tendentious; give me the* necessary references, citations, etc., *since you know that I have read neither Freud nor Lacan; I speak by 'hearsay' (of the first sort). All this so that I can take the time and find the means to rewrite this poorly turned out text in* theoretically cor-rect *French. In principle there is no rush.*"

The aforementioned addressees of this text (but perhaps he had sent it to still others, as was habitual with him) answered quite swiftly and in a detailed man-ner. In particular Jacques Nassif sent him a handwritten commentary of forty-five pages on July 1, and Elisabeth Roudinesco sent a typewritten text of sixteen pages, both of which analyze and criticize his text line by line, as he had asked.[2] All, with different arguments, confess their perplexity and agree on one point: in its state at the time his text was generally insufficient on the theoreti-cal level and consequently unpublishable—all, that is, with the exception of Fernand Deligny, who wrote to him, "To tell the truth, nothing in your 'hasty' text [. . .] offends me; quite the contrary," whereas he confessed to having been "offended, surprised, and disconcerted" by the article "Freud and Lacan." For his part, Michel Pêcheux opined that "The Discovery of Dr. Freud" resembles precisely a "settling of scores" with the article "Freud and Lacan," which "took a bit too much [. . .] the form of a liquidation," and alluding to the "health policies" of the French Communist Party, he emphasized that for those policies, "Lacan is irritating and for a long time already many have dreamed of 'taking him on' [. . .] because, ultimately and despite all his shenanigans, Lacan dis-turbs what you [Althusser] one day called the great family." He added, "What a divine surprise, then, what an unexpected gift for some: an 'Anti-Lacan' signed Althusser!"

Unsettled by these criticisms—which he gathered in a file called "Judgments 'Discovery of Dr. Freud' "—as may be seen from the numerous annotations he made on J. Nassif's text and above all by the letter he sent to E. Roudinesco on August 12 (which we publish in an appendix to "The Discovery of Dr. Freud"), Althusser wrote a second text, "On Marx and Freud," which was probably completed in December and which he then sent to Chertok, asking him to substitute it for the first one, which Chertok did. When the three vol-umes of the colloquium's official proceedings appeared in 1978,[3] however, al-though Althusser's text was indeed that of "On Marx and Freud," it was published under the title "The Discovery of Dr. Freud in its Relations with Marxist Theory," which could obviously result only in a confusion with the first *text, which had been withdrawn. It may also be remarked that several complete paragraphs of the text disappeared (see pp. 225, 239) in the proceedings of the Tbilisi colloquium. The contents of one of those withdrawn paragraphs, in which Althusser defends the idea that Freud's contribution to the exploration of the "figures of dialectic" can be considered as richer than that of Marx, suggest that the disappearance had every appearance of an act of censorship. Finally, it should be specified that Althusser ultimately did not go to the Tbilisi colloquium.*

Althusser subsequently published "On Marx and Freud" in German in 1977[4] and in Spanish in 1978,[5] but the text remained unpublished in France.

The "affair" properly speaking erupted only a few years later, in 1984, when Léon Chertok included in a special issue of the Revue de médecine psychosomatique *(no. 2 [1983]), then published and distributed by Editions Privat in Toulouse, several of the papers presented at the Tbilisi colloquium, notably (for France) those of Bernard Doray, Gérard Mendel, Léon Chertok, François Roustang, and . . . Louis Althusser. Sometime later, in the spring of 1984, Editions Privat distributed to bookstores, in a limited edition of several hundred copies,[6] a "book" entitled* Dialogues franco-soviétiques sur la psychanalyse, *which did no more than reproduce under a new cover that issue of the* Revue de médecine psychosomatique. *A note by Roland Jaccard in* Le Monde *of April 27, 1984, emphasized the interest of the publication and referred particularly to the "fascinating text of Louis Althusser: 'The Discovery of Dr. Freud,' which had not been presented at Tbilisi." Indeed, if one looks closely, one sees that one is dealing not with the text already published in the colloquium's official proceedings—as was the case for the other authors collected in the work—but with the first text ("The Discovery of Dr. Freud") sent by Althusser in June 1978 and then withdrawn and replaced a few months later by "On Marx and Freud," which would be published, it should be recalled, under the rather similar title "The Discovery of Dr. Freud in its Relations with Marxist Theory."*

What happened? Did Léon Chertok simply mistake his texts—as Catherine Clément would suppose and then take offense at in L'Ane?[7] *Or rather, exploiting in some way the confusion—whether deliberate or involuntary matters little—of titles, did he on his own authority publish the initial text, which Althusser had rejected? In point of fact, Althusser, on reviewing the journal, had issued a protest, by certified latter, to Editions Privat on February 27, 1984, indicating that Chertok had published his text without asking for his authorization and demanding consequently that his letter of protest be published in the following issue of the* Revue de médecine psychosomatique. *Sending a copy of his letter to Léon Chertok on the same day, he appended this brief note:*

The Tbilisi Affair

Dear Doctor,

I don't recognize you in this act of indelicacy. I am sending you a copy of my letter to Editions Privat.

Yours,

Louis Althusser

On March 1 the general editor of Editions Privat acknowledged to Louis Althusser receipt of his letter, presented him with "the apologies of the publisher, who was unaware of the specific modalities affecting the text emanating from you and published by us on the authorization of Dr. Chertok," and assured him that his letter would be published in the following issue of the journal. On April 20 Althusser wrote again to Editions Privat to ask that his protest be inserted as well in the volumes of the journal distributed in the form of the book Dialogues franco-soviétiques sur la psychanalyse. On that occasion he indicated what was in his eyes most serious in the "affair": "I am heartbroken at imposing on you these precautions and the expenses they will entail for you. I know that you played no role in it and that the indelicacy of the procedure lies entirely at Chertok's door. He was aware of everything; it was he who transmitted to the Soviets the text with which I replaced the initial one. I am all the more revolted in that I can't help assuming that Chertok must have been speculating on my withdrawal and my silence for four years, following the drama I went through, in order to dispense with asking for my agreement."[8] Roland Jaccard's note of praise in Le Monde of April 27 only reinforced Althusser in his condemnation of April 27 and provoked him—for the first time since 1980—to abandon his public silence,[9] addressing a letter (in which, on the whole, he repeated his arguments with Editions Privat) to François Bott, then editor-in-chief of Le Monde des livres:

Dear Sir,

I have read, in the literary section of Le Monde of April 27, a review, signed R. J., of a work, Dialogues franco-soviétiques, which Dr. Chertok compiled and had printed by Privat.

Dr. Chertok published in it, as he did in his Revue de médecine psychosomatique, a text of mine that, having judged it an unsuccessful, hastily written, and unpublishable draft, I had withdrawn from the Proceedings of the Tbilisi Congress, replacing it with another, which figures under my name in the Proceedings of the Congress.

In a letter to Privat, who will publish it in the next issue of Chertok's journal, I denounced the doctor's flagrant unscrupulousness. Taking sole charge of all the liaison work between the French and the Soviets and thus thoroughly informed of all aspects of this episode, Dr. Chertok, on his own initiative, violated every propriety and legal disposition and published my first text both in his journal and in his book. I assume that he thought it feasible to speculate on my withdrawal in order to make do without my authorization: he was well enough informed to be convinced that I would no more have given it to him today than seven years ago.

Out of respect for Editions Privat, I decided not to demand a confiscation of the publications in question. Editions Privat, moreover, will insert a note of protest in the book.

In order for your readers to be informed of what is a small scandal and of my position, I would be very obliged if you were willing to publish this clarification as soon as possible in your next literary section.

I have always appreciated the propriety of your newspaper, which is, in addition, in no way involved in this affair. Allow me to thank you in advance and to assure you, dear sir, of my esteem.

Louis Althusser

Le Monde *of May 11, 1984, thus published long excerpts of the letter in which an amusing misprint, bordering on parapraxis, may be found: the second paragraph ends with "which figures under his [instead of my] name in the Proceedings of the Congress."*[10] *The polemic ended publicly with Léon Chertok's reply to Louis Althusser in* Le Monde *of May 25:*

> I would like to make a few remarks about Monsieur Louis Althusser's letter concerning the text published under his name in Dialogues franco-soviétiques sur la psychanalyse.

> It is certainly not an "unsuccessful and hastily written draft." Those who read it will be able to realize that we are dealing with a carefully thought out and elaborated text. Monsieur Althusser deemed it wise to withdraw it at the time it was going to be given to the printer, substituting a text bearing a different title and whose content is completely different. Nothing could lead me to think that the first was definitively banned from publication by its author. If I took the initiative for which I am currently reproached, it is because I judged, on the contrary, that it was of the highest interest and deserved to be amply known.

With that response Léon Chertok only confirmed what an introductory note to "The Discovery of Dr. Freud" in the Revue de médecine psychosomatique, *attributed to the editor, had specified: "Written in 1977 and intended for a Soviet public, the following article was to appear in the collections published for purposes of discussion at the symposium on the unconscious held at Tbilisi in 1979. Although it was not possible, for a variety of reasons, to retain the article, we believe that it has lost nothing of its interest."*

It will be noted that neither in this reply to Le Monde nor in his introductory note does Léon Chertok question his right to publish a text without the authorization of its author. In the last analysis, the letter supplies an answer to the question we evoked earlier: behind an apparently benign manipulation of titles Chertok was deliberately engaging in a manipulation of texts, fully violating the right of literary property.

With the matter thus resolved, it has seemed imperative to us to present the reader with the two texts in question. It should be noted in passing that the Althusser archives contain two other, far shorter (but undated) versions of "On Marx and Freud," one of nine pages and the other of five, the latter explicitly written as the "summary" of the themes of his presentation, which suggests that at one point Althusser fully intended to go to Tbilisi. Nevertheless, because of the extremely confused publishing history of the two texts, we are publishing them from the typed versions retained by Althusser, specifying, when necessary, several significant variants from the published text.

O. C.

The Discovery of Dr. Freud

I would like to present a few observations about the relations between Freudian thought and what Freud calls the unconscious.

1. Freud never had the ambition of discovering the existence of unconscious phenomena. Those phenomena have existed for as long as humanity has existed, as can be seen from, among other phenomena, the interpretation of dreams, forms of possession, ceremonies of exorcism, and so on. This list is obviously not exhaustive.

What Freud satisfied himself with doing was affirming that unconscious phenomena are universally distributed in the existence of human individuals, in states of either wakefulness or sleep and whatever their activity (Freud left aside the question of knowing whether these phenomena might also affect nonhuman individuals). This point is quite important, since it means that manifestations of the unconscious[1] accompany all activities of human beings, whether they be conscious or unconscious (unconscious: the term is taken here not in the Freudian sense but in its most general sense: *nonconscious*).

2. Freud showed and affirmed that manifestations of the unconscious can occur *solely* in human subjects, thus in subjects *endowed with consciousness*. This point is extremely important since, given the universal character of effects of the unconscious, it means, *on the one hand*, that the unconscious is of a psychological or psychical nature and, *on the other hand*, that the unconscious plays a determining role in the constitution and functioning of what Freud calls the "psychical apparatus," which includes the unconscious, the preconscious, and *the conscious*.[2]

3. Freud showed and affirmed that the unconscious manifests it-

self[3] in a specific situation, bringing two conscious subjects into relation, a situation Freud called that of *transference*. In that situation one subject unconsciously projects onto the other certain elaborate forms of his unconscious phantasms and vice versa. Contrary to the existence of effects of the unconscious, which is universal, contrary to the determining role of the unconscious in the constitution and functioning of the psychical apparatus, which is universal, the relation of *transference* is not universal, or in any event, it does not attain the same degree of intensity. In addition the relation of transference, which can be instantaneous (as in the example of the "thunderbolt" of love at first sight), is not always instantaneous. In addition, finally, the relation of transference, when it exists, is not necessarily reciprocal: it can be relatively unilateral; that is, it can include or not include what Freud calls the countertransference, which is the transference of the second subject onto the first in response to the transference of the first subject onto the second.

4. We know that Freud reached these conclusions, which revolutionized psychology, following an extensive history marked above all by neurological investigations; then by his meeting Charcot and Bernheim, who practiced hypnosis, an encounter that gave Freud his first idea of transference and of the existence of an unconscious psyche (at the time Freud said "thought") in hysterics; and then by his collaboration with Breuer, who gave Freud the idea that one might treat hysterical symptoms other than through hypnosis and in a far more durable manner, by way of what Breuer called curiously a "talking cure." This entire development in Freud transpired under the philosophical influence of the energeticism of Ostwald, political economy, and the evolutionism of Darwin. Freud personally was a materialist and an atheist; he believed in the possibility of achieving scientific knowledge of reality, including psychical reality. Freud appears not to have had direct knowledge of Marx and Marxism, which he nevertheless never attacked.

5. I now move on to another point, of the greatest importance, which concerns not the recognition of the objective existence of effects of the unconscious and of their conditions but *the theory of the unconscious*. And on this point I will advance, with all due prudence, the following thesis: *despite his efforts, Freud did not succeed in elaborating a theory of the unconscious.* This thesis should be understood in its strongest sense: despite all his efforts, Freud did not succeed in elaborating a *sci-*

entific theory (in the sense of the sciences we know) of the unconscious. I add that Freud nevertheless furnished us with a considerable mass of materials, of unheard of richness, for constructing that theory but that he did not manage to construct it. I add that, up until this day, none of Freud's successors, despite all their efforts, has succeeded in constructing a *scientific* theory of the unconscious. We will have to ask ourselves why, when the right time comes.

6. All the materials Freud furnished us with come from the experience of analytic therapy.

What is analytic therapy? Therapy may be considered as an experimental situation particularly propitious for the production, control, and transformation of effects of the unconscious.

The fact that it is relatively artificial (we shall see to what rules it is subordinated) does not distinguish it from other experimental setups of known experimental sciences.

The experience of therapy confronts—in a single isolated room—the analyst and the analyzed. In Lacan's school the analyzed is now called the *analysand*, to give him the impression that he is "participating" in the therapy, but since he participates in it in any event, this is a lure, and Lacan, having elaborated the theory of lures and decoys, will not contradict me, unless it be to show that this lure is "gratifying," which runs counter to the thought and practice of Freud.

Therapy was subject to rules of great rigor:

a. first, to rules of *recruitment* of patients—the analyst having, like Charcot before him, to choose patients he is sure of being able to treat (in this case neurotics, but not psychotics) and of being able to treat without seriously disturbing the current balance of their psychical and social (conjugal, political, aesthetic, etc.) life;

b. then, to financial rules, the patient having to pay a contractual sum to his analyst, naturally aligned with any rise in the cost of living, should it occur—even if he misses (omission, forgetting, slip) a session;

c. then to a *commitment* on the part of the person being analyzed: he was obliged, as a humorist might write, to tell all with complete freedom, without self-control, and if need be, should he want to, not to say anything at all;

d. then to a *countercommitment* on the part of the analyst, who committed himself, for his part, to listen with neutral and "free-floating" benevolence to everything told him by the patient; and finally,

e. to a formal *refusal* by the analyst, whether made explicit or not:

the analyst refused in advance to act as a physician, that is, to give a diagnosis, to grant a prescription, to furnish any care whatsoever, or to take any decision whatsoever, even should the patient be in need of rest, internment, or protection against a suicidal impulse. Refusing to act as a physician, the analyst simultaneously refused to act as a confessor, counselor, or even as a friend.

With these rules clearly formulated (except for the last), the patient stretched out on a couch, the analyst kept in the background, outside the patient's field of vision but near enough to be able to hear him, and a long silence or a long monologue officially began. That was therapy. It was regulated in its duration (sessions of forty-five minutes to an hour) and in its rhythm (five to seven times a week).

The patient told everything that passed through his head, what came to his mind, what he had done, what he had not done, and why; he told his dreams if he had had any, and if he felt like it, he could also not say anything, go away before the end of the session, return for the next session, or not return at all. In the last case the analyst took on another patient.

In cases where things went well, that is, where the patient was faithful to his next session, the analyst observed that at a certain moment, the "transference" (between the patient and himself, of course) was established, established with sufficient solidity for serious work to begin.

There then intervened what Freud calls the "work" of therapy, or "work on the unconscious," "work" so difficult that Freud used a German word (*Durcharbeiten*) untranslatable in French to designate it. The analyst began by listening (analytic "listening"); then, when he felt that the moment had come, he intervened verbally to "interpret" this or that detail that he judged to be meaningful to show the patient, with infinite caution, that the detail could be understood only as a function of a primal fantasy more or less masked beneath the disguise of content that Freud dubbed "manifest" to oppose it to "latent" content (the manifest content was that of the dream recounted, of daily life recounted, in sum, of the patient's conscious thoughts, in opposition to the "latent" content, which formed the patient's "unconscious thoughts"). And so forth.

This work was pursued until the end of the therapy, which was always difficult, indeed very difficult, for there occurred in it what Freud came at the end of his life to call the "countertransference," effected this time by the analyst on the patient, which the analyst had not had the wit to notice previously. In general this countertransference is a countertransference of introjective identification, which means that the analyst cannot manage to separate himself from the patient, that is, from the idea he has of the role he is playing in the patient's life.

7. It is on the basis of the very rich material gathered in the experimental situation of various cases of therapy (with, it is true, the restriction that the same situation can never be reproduced, since on each occasion either the patient or the analyst is a new and consequently different individual), thus on the conscious and unconscious material furnished by patients in their therapy, and thus also on the interpretations furnished by analysts to their patient, on the occasion of the analysis of such material—it is on this basis that Freud constructed, rather late, it is true, *what he believed to be a scientific psychological theory of the unconscious* that he consequently called *metapsychology*, a word we may consider to be a theoretical confession and diagnosis.

It is plainly not a matter of *reproaching* Freud for not having written what he did not write, with not having done what, by his own admission, moreover (he was quite prudent in theoretical matters), he neither did nor was able to do. It is not a matter of reproaching Freud with not having furnished a *scientific* theory of the unconscious, that is, a theory of the mechanisms (whatever they be) producing effects of the unconscious observed by Freud and observable by anyone, not only in analytic therapy, but in daily life, be it private or social.

On the other hand, it is important for us to know exactly what Freud did and what he did not do. In particular, it is important for us to know that Freud discovered new conditions of manifestation, control, and transformation of effects of the unconscious in human subjects, and that in itself is already a prodigious thing, without which we would still be stuck with Charcot and Bernheim, thus with hypnosis, which never yields lasting results, unless they be, precisely, pathological results.

And it is quite important for us to know what Freud did not do. Why? In order to avoid theoretical misunderstandings, which prove either the good will or the bad faith of certain individuals but which, in any event, prove only one thing: their ignorance of Freud. The problem is that such an ignorance of Freud, decked out as a false Freudian theory of the unconscious, necessarily provokes chain effects not only among analysts and their patients but among all who are quite rightly interested in Freud and in analysis.

8. To illustrate what I have just said, I shall take a first example, that of a certain tendency said to form part of American psychoanalysis (I specify "said to form part of American psychoanalysis" since this tendency is not specific to the American analytic school, and there are, in North America, which is being targeted here, tendencies quite different from this one) that reduces analytic work to what it calls the "analysis of defenses" and the "reinforcement of the ego."

J. Lacan has had the great merit of criticizing this false interpretation of the thought and practice of Freud. I will thus not linger over it. Let us say that this interpretation of Freud represents a regressive deviation: it causes Freud's thought to fall back into psychology, that is, into a branch of morality, and—something inevitable but serious—into practices amounting to the social retraining of the individual. Lacan is completely correct: nothing is further than that interpretation and practice from the spirit and practice of Freud, which, as all know, always revealed a great attachment to the freeing of individuals and refused to treat them in order to subject them to social readaptation. It is not without interest to see that in the history of psychoanalysis in the Soviet Union, until 1930, an entire tendency defended that great lesson of Freud's against another tendency that wanted to place psychoanalysis in the service of the new values of the revolution.

9. To illustrate what I have just said, I shall take a second example, that of Lacan himself. We all know what we owe to J. Lacan, a great French psychiatrist, who has resolutely—and for a long time in utter solitude—waged fierce ideological combat for an acknowledgement of the "*Freudian thing*," that is, the specificity of Freud's thought, and for the respect of the values to which Freud was most attached: materialism, atheism, freedom.

And yet J. Lacan was not satisfied with that struggle, which might have filled a man's life. He attempted to do what Freud had been unable to do: *he attempted to constitute a scientific theory of the unconscious.* To that end, as everyone knows, he sought support in the linguistics of Saussure and the authors of the Prague school, above all Jakobson. In addition Lacan attempted to think through, in the strong sense, that is, in the scientific sense, what Freud left us. He did it thanks to a hypothesis of great daring by writing this simple sentence: "*the unconscious is structured like a language.*" Now Freud, who knew what was up when it came to the unconscious, had never written that. But why not try? Lacan thus continued by constituting a whole theory distinguishing the real, the symbolic, and the imaginary. Freud, who knew what was up when it came to the unconscious, had never resorted to such a theory, in which all is conceived not as a function of the unconscious but as a function of the *symbolic*, that is, of language and the law and thus of the "name of the father." Freud had never spoken of the name of the father, and so on. I cannot enter here into the details of a gigantic edifice that has not stopped proliferating, and for good reason, which is that it could only pursue an object that was out of its reach because it did not exist. What did not exist was the *possibility today* to constitute a *scientific* theory of the unconscious. That possibility will perhaps exist tomorrow, and if it exists, it will take on forms that will certainly surprise Lacan himself, but that possibility does not exist today.

What, then, did Lacan do? He set out in search of a scientific theory of the unconscious; he decided to do what Freud had been unable to do—and instead of offering a scientific theory of the unconscious, he gave an astonished world *a philosophy of psychoanalysis*. I say a philosophy of psychoanalysis in the sense in which Engels, speaking about the philosophy of nature, the philosophy of history, and so on, said that those disciplines have no right to exist because they have no object. The old Kantian lesson that there can exist what Kant called "sciences without object" (like rational theology, cosmology, and psychology) and that are nothing but philosophies without objects (and that is correct, for philosophy has no object) had been forgotten by Lacan, despite the reminder by Engels and several other Marxists. He had produced a fantastic philosophy of psychoanalysis that has fascinated intellectuals for decades throughout the world, whether they be analysts or not. It has fascinated them for two reasons: first because Lacan in his way is a philosopher of strong thought, which is delicately concealed behind an esoteric façade, and then because Lacan was speaking about psychoanalysis. Lacan was thus playing a double game. To philosophers he brought the guarantee of the master who is "supposed to know" what Freud thought. To psychoanalysts he brought the guarantee of the master who is "supposed to know" what thinking (philosophically) means. He duped everybody, and quite plausibly, despite his extreme trickiness, he duped himself as well. I shall give but a single proof of this. In his famous seminar on the purloined letter, after a meticulous and intriguing analysis of Poe's text, Lacan concludes, "according to which *a letter always arrives at its destination*." It is a line excessively encumbered with meanings and echoes in a philosophy of the signifier, the letter, the unconscious as signifier. To that declaration, which is supported by a whole philosophy not of the addressee [*destinataire*] but of destiny or fate, and thus of the most classical finality, I will simply oppose the materialist thesis: *it happens* [il arrive] *that a letter does not arrive at its destination.*

As for the question of knowing what sort of philosophy Lacan may have fabricated while drawing simultaneously on Freud and on linguistics, and then on formal logic and mathematics, it is a question that would take us away from our subject. I will simply note that considered in its most general bearing, Lacan's philosophy, which flirted with Heidegger for a long while, appears to me to fall, in the final analysis, less under the rubric of structuralism, which is but a variant of it, than under that of formal logic. I am giving my impression of an oeuvre that is, moreover, baroque, philosophically uncertain, and that has had to pay the price *in philosophy* for the uncertainty in which Lacan found himself in relation to the object he claimed to be thinking in order to forge a *scientific* theory of the unconscious. When a philosophy is constituted as a philosophy in order to think the object of a science not yet in existence, there is in fact every reason to think that the philosophy is teetering on the pedestal of its uncertain theses.

10. I return to Freud simply to register an observation. Freud did not give us a scientific theory of the unconscious. He gave us something else, however: not only a theory of the analytic material collected in the course of therapy but a prodigiously moving attempt to *think through* the result of his experiences. The fact that this thought did not manage to attain the form of a scientific theory is one thing. It nonetheless remains a prodigiously capacious body of thought, in the strong sense, and this is the most important point, one that is prodigiously attentive to every detail, curious about every novelty, and in *perpetual motion.* It is indeed quite remarkable, and it has not been sufficiently noted, that Freud never stopped, until the last days of his life, recasting his thought, his concepts, and what he himself called his general "hypotheses." If he never stopped *recasting* his thought, it was because he had not arrived at a scientific theory establishing systematized and homogeneous definitive results of the following type (I ask forgiveness for this modest example, but it is irrefutable and clear): $2 + 2 = 4$. On the other hand, if he never stopped *recasting* his thought, it was because he never accepted the thought that he had achieved a definitive—that is, *scientific*—result on which he had but to work in or-

der to produce new and true forms of knowledge. No. For Freud no result was ever definitive. The proof is that he never stopped changing his basic hypotheses, not the existence of the unconscious and its manifestations (he never doubted their "reality"), but the theoretical expression of that existence.

On the other hand, those who believed that Freud had forged a scientific theory of the unconscious, like Adler or Jung, took their distance from Freud and began fabricating *philosophies of the unconscious* that had but little to do not only with Freud's thought but with the whole set of facts gathered by Freudian practice; they became blind to the facts themselves. In their philosophy of the unconscious, however, they started with a philosophical theory as constituting the equivalent of a scientific theory, a definitive fundamental result from which one must start in order to obtain new results. And they did not stop raving theoretically, separating themselves more and more from the facts.

On the other hand, someone like Lacan, who believed that Freud had discovered the scientific theory of the unconscious without knowing it and that it was enough to add to that content the form it was lacking, also formally proceeded in the same manner, *with this difference*: he produced (unlike Adler and Jung) not a necessarily delusional philosophy from the theoretical point of view but *a philosophy of psychoanalysis* in general that has remained far closer to Freud's thought, to his writings, and to the analytic material. But Lacan also proceeded *as though he had attained an indisputable scientific result*, in a theoretical form he had forged for that result, and he constantly worked on the basis of what he considered to be an indisputable scientific theoretical achievement to derive new theoretical conclusions from it. In point of fact, we know that his theoretical conclusions were only philosophical.

But that is why it is imperative, in contrast, to insist on the extraordinary character of Freud's thought. He never considers the theoretical "hypotheses" he proposes to be definitive. He cannot do without them, since he is attempting to think in the strong sense what he does and what he observes, but never does he think he has a definitive hypothesis, that is, a truly scientific hypothesis. That is why he changes hypotheses—and does so until the end of his life. Paradoxically the most profound proof of Freud's genuinely scientific spirit, his criticism, his antidogmatism, is revealed in his instinctive reluctance to describe as *scientific* in the strong sense the provisional formulations he arrives at in accounting for facts that are nonetheless indisputable and that converge in the most impressive manner.

I think that a rereading of the whole of Freud's work starting from the hypothesis I have just enunciated would finally allow one to understand the *necessity of the paradox* of a body of thought that is deeply scientific but at the same time prodigiously prudent, a thought that is unperturbable but at the same time multifarious, a thought that never stops saying the same thing, deepening it, but that at the same time says it in forms that are new at every turn and at every turn disconcerting. It is on the condition of approaching Freud's thought with that explanatory hypothesis in mind that it is possible to see what Freud brought us that was definitive, even if the form he gave to that definitive contribution was not that of a scientific theory in the strong sense.

11. There are, in point of fact, a certain number of "nuclei" in Freud's thought that never varied.

First there is the theme of *infantile sexuality*. The results of work with and on hypnosis, first, and then the results of therapy, such as the analysis of dreams, quickly brought to light the existence of a reality that was literally scandalous for Freud's contemporaries. That reality, which is still scandalous, is the existence of an infantile sexuality in ultradeveloped form, that is, a form infinitely more developed than adult sexuality, to such an extent that Freud could say that the child, as opposed to the adult, is a "polymorphous pervert."

Infantile sexuality, the child's "polymorphous perversity," is not a hypothesis; it is a fact. Any alert observer can experience it with the nursing babies, infants, and small children of his surroundings. Contrary to an entire moral ideology of the child, the world of little children is spontaneously and naturally fascinated and obsessed by observable *sexual practices*. If that simple fact, which is observable by anyone in his surroundings, was denied for so long, Freud interprets it by saying that it was the object of a form of censorship. In addition Freud says that the unconscious is necessarily related to the effect of that censorship: *repression*.

But Freud did not speak only of observable (and thus objective) infantile sexuality. He spoke also of the *subjective sexuality* of babies and children, which is understandable, since one would be hard put to imagine that sexual practices—above all by very young children and even by babies—might take place without corresponding to *wishes*, which would obviously be unconscious at that age.

Freud, still reasoning quite simply but all the more forcefully, thus came to conclude *the existence of an unconscious sexuality linked to unconscious wishes.*

Now what is quite remarkable for us in this discovery is that contrary to what we might believe, Freud did not discover things in the order in which I just set them forth. Freud did not proceed from the observation of the objective sexuality of babies and small children to the idea of their subjective unconscious sexuality, and thus to the idea of their unconscious sexual wish; on the contrary, Freud discovered (by way of the material gathered in *adult* therapy!) the existence of unconscious sexual wishes in the small child, and it was on the basis of that hypothesis that the existence of objective sexual practices in the baby and small child began to be observed. We have by now acquired the habit of considering all that as natural, including the order of Freud's discovery, despite his fantastic paradox (since Freud went, against all experimental practice, from the unseen, the nonobservable—the child's unconscious sexual wishes—to the seen, the observable—the sexual practices of little children and infants), but in Freud's day none of this was natural; on the contrary, it was all "morally" scandalous. Worse yet, it was "scientifically" scandalous to move from what is not objectively observable to the objectively observable, unless it be admitted, something Freud was convinced of, that what is not directly observable (namely, the existence of unconscious sexual wishes in the very small child on the basis of adult analyses) was itself, if not directly observable, at least identifiable in the practice of therapy, that is, in the analysis of those same adults.

12. The first nucleus is thus the theme of unconscious infantile sexuality and consequently the existence of unconscious "thought" or unconscious "wishes" in every individual.

The second nucleus, revealed by the first, is the idea of a prodigious social *censorship* of those same unconscious sexual wishes. I say *social* since it was enough for Freud to announce publicly his discovery of unconscious sexual wishes in earliest infancy for all the powers that be, from psychology and medicine to morality, religion, and politics, to rise with violence against his discovery. One would have thought oneself at the time of the Holy Inquisition condemning Galileo. But that is not what is most important; if all those powers in concert rose up against Freud, it was because until then, that is, in the whole of human history before Freud, they had succeeded in censoring by intimidation and blackmail the idea that the facts discovered by Freud, which had always existed, *might exist*. But that is not what is most important. If there existed in society that prodigious force of social censorship bearing on the precise point of the existence of unconscious sexual wishes in the small child, it was unthinkable that the small child, that all small children, would be able to escape the effect of that prodigious censorship. Whence Freud's idea that the unconscious sexual wishes of the small child encounter not only in society (of which he is unaware) but also in his own psyche the phantasmatic effects of that censorship: repression. Whence Freud's idea that this force of repression of unconscious sexual wishes in the small child *is also an unconscious force*.

The most astonishing aspect, once again, is that in arriving at his result, Freud did not follow the path I just indicated. He did not start out from the observation of objective social repression (exercised by the ideological apparatuses of the state that I just mentioned: family, school, church, etc.). Quite to the contrary, it was in the analysis of material furnished by therapy that he found, in the strong sense, observed, discovered, the existence of unconscious repression exercising its power of intimidation, blackmail, and interdiction over the unconscious sexual wishes of the small child. There, too, the path followed by Freud was "scientifically" scandalous, going from the inside to the outside, from the unseen to the seen, from the unobservable to the observable, with the reservation that Freud could say—and he was entirely correct—that he was able to observe *in a completely objective manner* within the experimental practice of therapy, if not the existence of the unconscious in person, at least the existence of effects of the unconscious. In addition, as a good materialist scientist, since he observed effects, being convinced that those effects could not exist without a "cause," he attributed a cause to them, even if he could not see it. In that he was in very good scientific company, since all physicists, chemists, and biologists can construct their science only by presupposing the existence of causes that they nonetheless *cannot see*. Better still, it is in hypothesizing the existence of a cause they do not manage to see *that they manage to see it*. When they succeed in seeing it, however, the cause that they see is always different from the cause that they anticipated seeing. The cause of the effects is in perpetual flight from science, and that, moreover, is what motivates all sciences, subjectively, to live.

Freud knew all that, which is why he always compared himself to a researcher in the *natural* sciences—not to a mathematician or a logician, as Lacan likes to do—and he was 100 percent right. He even compared himself so well to a researcher in the natural sciences that he was convinced—and he never stopped saying as much—that one day psychoanalysis would be united with neurology, biochemistry, and chemistry. For Freud knew that his discovery could become *the object of a natural science* (I recall here that Marx says that historical materialism ought to be considered for what it is, a "natural science," for history is part of nature, since nothing else exists in the world except nature). Nonetheless, Freud also knew that one does not *decree* that a discovery *has become* a science. He knew that certain objective conditions must be satisfied for that transformation of a discovery of nature to be possible. He knew that those conditions were not extant in his day. I will add that they are not present in our day but that there exist serious hopes stemming from recent developments in the neuro-bio-chemistry of the human body and brain, on the one hand (an aspect anticipated by Freud), and from historical materialism, on the other (an aspect that Freud could not intuit). Experience shows that a discovery becomes a science only when it can establish *theoretical links* between its own discovery and other existing sciences. This is what one sees happening, for example, in biology with the discovery of DNA. The discoveries of biology became a science the day on which a theoretical connection could be made between those discoveries and another science, in this case, biochemistry. That link was constituted in principle (for much remains to be discovered) through the discovery of DNA. The same will occur for the discoveries of Freud, but things will certainly be more complicated.

13. I return to Freud and the existence of unconscious sexual wishes or desires in the small child. Whoever speaks of desire obviously must speak of the object of that desire. To speak of sexual desire is obviously to speak of a sexual object.

Now who are the sexual objects of the unconscious sexual wishes or desires of the small child? Those close to him and himself. From there (and I note that for clarity of exposition, I am once more obliged to follow the inverse order of the one followed by Freud in his experimentation), one can understand the entire "theory" of infantile sexuality as Freud presented it. The small child takes himself as a sexual object (the oral and anal stages), but at the same time he also takes his mother as a sexual object, and taking his mother as a sexual object, he will end up, after a certain time (when what Freud calls the "Oedipal relation" will be formed), *also* taking his father as a sexual object—but in order to wish unconsciously for his death, for he wants his mother for himself alone, and since his mother belongs to his father, he wants the death of his father. All that transpires in the unconscious sexual wishes of the small child. It is a truth known by everyone for a long time, however, despite social censorship, since a poet named Sophocles put the conflict on stage, since a writer named Diderot, who could not have known Freud, tranquilly wrote that every little child "wants to sleep with his mother and kill his father," a sentence that had gone unperceived but that Freud noted (one understands why).

What is fascinating in this whole dialectic is that the parents, just like the little child, are objective social beings, whom anyone can see, touch, and hear, whose objective behavior can be observed, and whose objective behavior can be studied on the basis of the scientific principles of historical materialism.

What is still more fascinating in this whole story is that what occurs in the unconscious sexual wishes of the little child necessarily has objective relations with the objective familial situation. No one any longer doubts this except those whose scientific intelligence is limited by their moral, religious, or political will. But the fact that there are objective relations, and it is clear that there are, is one thing; it is another thing to arrive at a *scientific theory* of those relations. Freud never claimed to be able to elaborate the scientific theory of those relations. He was too modest, that is, too aware of the existing conditions of impossibility to have that ambition. At least he observed the existence of those relations, however, and he was absolutely convinced (as is demonstrated by his books—even if they are not very good or if they are bad—on what he called "civilization," namely, *Totem and Taboo* and *The Future of an Illusion*) that those *relations existed* and that one had to take them into account if one wanted one day to explain scientifically the effects of the unconscious. Freud was a genuine scientific investigator: he took into account *all* the conditions of existence of the object of his research. That is why, contrary to Lacan, who speaks very little about it, too little, contrary to Reich, who speaks *only* about it, Freud took into greatest account the existence of the family, of morality, of religion, and so on, in sum, of what I call in my language the effects on the small child, and thus on the unconscious sexual wishes of the small child and on their unconscious repression, of the existence of state ideological apparatuses.

14. From there, one can understand how Freud's thought developed. After the oral and anal stages (in which the small child takes himself as the object of his unconscious sexual desire) comes the genital stage, in which the small child explicitly and openly takes another person (passing from a "component object" to a "total object") as the object of his unconscious sexual desire: his mother. And taking his mother as his sexual object, he moves to the genital stage, which, except in cases of regression, is the one in which his entire life as a young child, an adolescent, and then an adult will take place. But we know that the counterpart to his unconscious sexual desires' fixation on his mother is the hatred of the father, who then appears as representing censorship, as the origin of repression. The child then lives in that curious *tripartite contradiction* that Freud calls the Oedipus complex. He must "phantasmatically" kill his father to be able to possess his mother as object of his sexual desire, but since he cannot really kill his father, he will phantasmatically "internalize" his father, that is, establish him in his unconscious as a distinct figure, that of repressive censorship. This is the origin of what Freud calls the *superego*. When he succeeds in the difficult "negotiation" that Freud calls the "liquidation of the Oedipus complex" (and he does not always succeed at it, whence come the neuroses and certain psychoses), the child manages in some manner to make peace with his father in order to obtain from him permission to possess unconsciously his mother. That peace transacted with the father is called the appearance of the superego. The child has succeeded in "internalizing," and thus in part in disarming, that "agency" of social and phantasmatic censorship represented by the "imago" of the father. He has succeeded in "making peace" with the unconscious phantasmatic imago of the father and thus with himself, with his contradictory unconscious sexual desires, and with their strange tripartite contradiction. He can advance in life armed with that strength, which can be quite fragile.

That peace, however, that pact, represents for him his sole chance of one day becoming "a man like daddy," possessing "a woman like mommy," and being able to desire her and possess her not only unconsciously but consciously and publicly, either in marriage or in the freedom of a love relation, when the state of the society's laws allows it. I say that this strength can be quite fragile because if the Oedipus complex has not been negotiated sufficiently well, if the peace (which in truth is never completely achieved) has not been suitably realized in the child's unconscious, elements of contradiction subsist in the child's unconscious that then give rise to what Freud calls *neurotic* formations. As for the *psychoses*, Freud thought that they stem from a period prior to the Oedipus complex: to the extent that the negotiation of the Oedipus complex remains incomplete, the psychotic child, and then the psychotic (that is, mad) man, remains fixated on pre-Oedipal object relations that quickly end up entering into contradiction with the demands of reality (which Freud calls the "reality principle") and thus denying reality, which provokes the well-known phenomenon of the "splitting of the ego" (*Ichspaltung*), which Lacan, misreading Freud, thought defined every "subject of the unconscious," whereas Freud never spoke either of the "subject of the unconscious" or, obviously, of the unconscious as a "subject."

From there one can understand the extraordinary import of Freudian thought. What Freud discovered applies to all human beings, not merely to nurselings and small children but also to adolescents and adults, not merely to individuals of the male sex but to individuals of the female sex (in little girls, the Oedipus complex has a slightly more complicated form, since the object to be eliminated is the mother, but the mother is at the same time the first object of sexual desire, and in the case of the feminine Oedipus complex, *she is not the representative of the repressive censor*, it's the father who represents the censor, the cause of unconscious repression, and it is he who is desired unconsciously by the little girl; she desires, in sum, he who forbids all desire), not merely to overtly sexed individuals but also to homosexuals and all perverts, and not only to neurotics but also to psychotics.

The ingenious paradox of Freudian thought is that Freud opened up all those paths *solely* through the experimentation of therapy with ordinary subjects who came to see him because "things weren't going well in their lives." And all that transpired in the peaceful consulting room of a Viennese Jewish physician who was satisfied to open his door to his patients at a fixed time and let them stretch out on a couch and listen to them.

15. But the most mind-boggling paradox of Freud's thought is no doubt that Freud *opened up all those paths* without truly entering onto them himself. Freud analyzed only adults. He never analyzed a small child. It is known that little Hans was "analyzed" . . . by his father,

whom Freud advised. Nonetheless, since Freud child psychoanalysis has taken giant strides and has completely confirmed Freud's predictions. For example, Freud never analyzed a psychotic properly speaking, even if one can consider Anna O. to have been a psychotic, but it was precisely *her* therapy that failed, plunging Freud into perplexity and despair. As for President Schreber, Freud did not analyze him; he analyzed his writings, which is not the same thing. An analysis is never conducted by correspondence, for we know, despite what Lacan says, that in such cases letters *never* reach their destination. To succeed, an analysis, I regret to say, must exclude every *letter* to be able to make use of it. Nevertheless, since Freud's time there has been a broad evolution in the analysis of psychotics—which is terribly difficult, since the "splitting of the ego" makes a transference practically impossible, and one has to resort to unprecedented practical ruses to succeed (certain analysts have a kind of genius in this domain, as do other people, above all people who are not official analysts, since to be an official analyst, burdened with the rules of therapy, generally impedes one from inventing untried forms, always new, that allow the transference with a psychotic to be established). In the same way the analysis of homosexuals and perverts has evolved. All the experience accumulated since Freud has completely verified his hypotheses.

If one asks oneself how it could be that a man who was initially alone and then helped by a few friends and disciples, the best of whom abandoned him to found non-Freudian schools, a man who never had before himself anything but patients selected from among adult neurotics, was thus able to open the paths of the psychoanalysis of children, psychotics, homosexuals, and perverts, one is plainly asking an unheard of question, and one is tempted to believe in a miracle. Indeed Freud, who was detested like all the great discoverers, was also the object of a kind of cult that insisted on the miraculous omnipotence of his thought.

Nevertheless, Freud himself gave us the secret of that "miracle." He simply said that *the unconscious is extremely poor*. In saying that, he was simultaneously saying the truth and a very simple thing. He meant that the unconscious is poor because it is *simple*. It is simple because it is constituted by a small number of elements that I enumerated in my talk, and the fact is that one can count on the fingers of both hands those basic elements, which are limited in number. To say that the basic elements of the unconscious are simple does not at all mean that your unconscious and mine are simple: on the contrary, they are complicated, extraordinarily complicated. Their complication stems from the way in which those simple elements (which can each possess a greater or lesser degree of intensity, which Freud calls "affect") are combined. Once one knows that the affect can vary from zero to infinity, one sees that the possible combinations are infinite and thus infinitely varied. That is why no unconscious resembles another unconscious.

It is because of the "poverty," however, that is, the simplicity of the elements in play, that Freud, with a facility that may have seemed to be supernatural, was able to *anticipate both* the existence of problems he had not himself experienced *and* the theoretical and practical solution of those problems. In that regard he did not do anything that distinguishes him from other researchers in the natural sciences and historical materialism, who, precisely like Freud, are able, on the basis of the elements at their disposition (and they are always limited in number; no biologist, physicist, or chemist will say otherwise), to open up paths that they do not know and that are subsequently recognized by their successors.

16. I will not go any further in this domain. The reader can pursue things on his own, given the simplicity of matters. To finish things, however, I would like to return to what I said earlier, namely, that Freud could not claim—*because he knew* that he could not do it—to have produced a *scientific* theory of the unconscious.

That recognition is everywhere inscribed in Freud's work, and if I may say so, *is spelled out*, which quite proves that the letters thus spelled out did not arrive at their destined recipients and that in particular, Lacan, who claims some expertise when it comes to letters and recipients, did not receive his, which was lost in transit, even if he had it under his eyes.

In order not to abuse the reader's patience, I shall restrict my analysis to two of Freud's concepts.

I take up the concept of *drive* first. It is quite an interesting concept, for Freud never managed to give a satisfying definition of it, which did not prevent the concept from "functioning" quite suitably within metapsychological "theory" and in practice. Why this impossibility in defining it? Not because of its imprecision but because of the impossibility of thinking its precision theoretically. This concept seeks its definition in an impossible difference with instinct, that is, with a biological reality. I say impossible since for Freud, the drive (*Trieb*) is profoundly bound to a biological reality, even though it is distinct from it. Freud extricates himself by saying that the drive (which is always sexual) is like a "representative" of the somatic within the psychical, is *"a limit concept between the somatic and the psychical."* That indication is precise, but at the same time one sees that, to think it, Freud is forced to resort to a metaphor ("representative") or to think not the thing but the concept itself! ("a limit concept between the somatic and the psychical"), which clearly amounts to acknowledging the impossibility of thinking scientifically the object that is nonetheless designated with great clarity. It is, moreover, quite remarkable that the region beyond this "limit" designates biological reality, from which will surely come, in conjunction with the reality known by historical materialism, the discoveries that will one day allow the elaboration of the scientific theory of the unconscious.

Finally, I address the concept of *phantasm.* We encountered it when I said that the child wanted "phantasmatically" to kill his father or lovingly possess his mother. This signifies to all appearances that the phantasm designates something other than objective reality, an other—no less objective—reality, although it does not appear to the senses. (Freud writes: "Should we acknowledge a *reality* in unconscious wishes? I am incapable of saying. . . . When one is confronted with unconscious wishes reduced to their ultimate and truest expression, one is indeed obliged to say that *psychical reality* is a particular form of existence that should not be confused with *material* reality.") The phantasm is thus a reality sui generis. The phantasm is linked to desire. The phantasm is unconscious. The phantasm is a kind of "fantasy," of "scenario," of *"mise en scène,"* in which something serious happens and in which nothing happens, for all transpires in an extreme affective tension (the affect) that literally congeals the characters (the "imagos"), which are also phantasms, in their reciprocal positions of desire or interdiction. One thus sees that the phantasm is *contradictory,* since something occurs in it, but nothing happens; that everything is immobile, but in an intense form of tension that is the very opposite of immobility, in which everything is desire and all is interdiction; and finally, one sees that the phantasm is a totality composed of phantasms, that is, of itself, of its own null repetition. One rediscovers in all this fundamental themes of Freud's thought: namely, *the repetition instinct,* specific to the unconscious, and the *complete indifference* of the unconscious concerning the *principle of contradiction.* One reaches the most elaborated point of the Freudian theory of the unconscious at this juncture. *The concept of the phantasm is nothing other, in Freud, than the concept of the unconscious in all its extension and all its comprehension.* We are obliged to observe that in the phantasm Freud designates something extremely precise, an exis- tent—though nonmaterial—reality, concerning which no misunder- standing is possible, and a material reality that is the very existence of its object: the unconscious. But we are also obliged to observe that the name Freud gives to that reality, in other words, the name Freud gives to the unconscious when he attains the zenith of his theory in order to think it, is the name of a *metaphor*: phantasm.

Taking up Freud's phrase about the drive, a limit concept between the somatic and the psychical, I will say that the concept of the phan- tasm in Freud is at once the concept of the unconscious, but not its *sci- entific* concept, since it is a metaphor, although it can, on the other hand, be *for us* the concept *of the limit* that separates a theoretical for- mation that has not yet become a science from the science to come. For, thank God, between that theoretical formation and science there is at least a little phantasm, the illusion of having attained science, and, since the phantasm is contradictory, a bit of genuine desire to finally reach it.

17. As Marx said, we will not have to await the consequences for long. As Spinoza said, we have all our time to discover eternal verities. Which is the same thing.

Appendix

Letter to Elisabeth Roudinesco following her commentary on "The Discovery of Dr. Freud"

We publish here the letter sent by L. Althusser to E. Roudinesco after receiving from her a detailed critique of the "first draft" of his article "The Discovery of Dr. Freud," initially sent to Léon Chertok for the Tbilisi colloquium. [4]

Gordes, 12/8/76

My dear Elisabeth:

What a pleasure to read your savory, lucid, and generous critique! I thank you for having taken time from your vacation to read me and correct my blunders.

In any event, you give me what I need to revise the text, if ever I do it, since so many others can speak of Freud better than I. It remains that I was writing for the Tbilisi Soviets, with a few thoughts in the back of my mind about distortions in need of being set aright. But that doesn't explain everything, since, as you know, I am ignorant in Freudian and Lacanian theory, except through hearsay, and I am overcome with admiration at the number of people who, at present, know.

What remains, once one has taken into account all these lapses, is the question of Lacan, which I also had in mind, even though I dealt with it in part by pretending not to. You say that you have made your choice and do not impose your path on anyone. Will you allow me in turn to object that this claim is a bit facile? It is a matter not of denying all that one owes to Lacan but of judging the effects by the causes; they are frequently null or of consummate confusion, which is more serious, null in that they lead to an impasse and are sterile (a bit the Picasso of psychoanalysis, not the Gongora), and even if I am too severe, you won't deny that one is steeped in malaise and ambiguity and that the "philosophy" that ends up in the waters of neopositivism is not very reassuring. At the very least it seems to me that if failure to judge Lacan leads one to treat him as a symptom himself, then one ought to conclude that one should all the same manage to state what he might be the symptom of, perhaps of something that Freud did not exactly get right, be it in his object, his concepts, or simply his language, since Lacan has felt the need to transform it, not without reason. Well, we'll speak about all this when I am better acquainted with the texts, which I know too poorly to counter you with them.

Nassif, to whom I showed my pages, sent me a critique of sixty handwritten pages, which more or less overlap with yours, although with more question marks, and he is finally rather prudent with regard to my reservations about Lacan. A sign of the times?

Have a good end of your vacation, dear Elisabeth, and consider yourself thanked from the bottom of my heart for your letter and your friendship. I embrace you.

Louis

On Marx and Freud

There is currently broad agreement, despite symptomatic resistances whose causes should be examined, in acknowledging that, in the domain of the "social" or "human sciences," two unprecedented and to-tally unforeseeable discoveries completely upset the universe of cultural values of the "classical age," that of the rise and settling into power of the bourgeoisie (from the sixteenth to the nineteenth century). The discoveries in question are those of historical materialism, namely, the theory of the conditions, forms, and effects of the class struggle, the work of Marx, and that of the unconscious, the work of Freud. Prior to Marx and Freud culture rested on the diversity of the *sciences* of nature, completed by various *ideologies* or philosophies of history, society, and the "human subject." With Marx and Freud *scientific* theories suddenly begin to occupy "regions" that until then had been reserved for theoretical formations of bourgeois *ideology* (political economy, sociology, psychology) or rather occupy, within those "regions," surprising and disconcerting positions.

There is, however, also broad agreement in acknowledging that the phenomena treated by Marx and Freud, namely, the effects of the class struggle and the effects of the unconscious, were not unknown before them. An entire tradition of political philosophers, and before them those "practitioners" evoked by Spinoza in reference to Machiavelli—who spoke directly about class struggle and to whom we owe the thesis of the priority of contradiction over contraries, the best known being the philosophers of natural law, who spoke indirectly about it beneath a cloak of juridical ideology—had recognized, well before Marx, the existence of classes and effects of class struggle. Marx himself acknowledged as his direct ancestors, from whom he took his distance through the critique he elaborated of the bourgeois theory of the class struggle, the bourgeois historians of the Restoration and the economists of the school of Ricardo, such as Hodgskin: those authors had recognized the existence of classes and of class struggle. Similarly the effects of the unconscious that Freud studied had been partially recognized in earliest antiquity, in dreams, prophesies, phenomena of possession and exorcism, and so on sanctioned by precise treatments.

In this sense neither Marx nor Freud *invented* anything: the object whose theory each produced existed before their discoveries. What each man did contribute was the definition of his object, its limits and extension, the characterization of its conditions and its forms of existence and effects, the formulation of the requirements that need be fulfilled to apprehend it and act on it: in brief, its theory, or the initial forms of its theory.

There is nothing that is not commonplace in that remark, if it be true that for materialism, every discovery does no more than produce the form of knowledge of an object already existing "outside thought."

Things become more interesting, however, when the conditions of those disconcerting discoveries *completely renew the conditions previously recognized as normal for all discoveries*. It is no doubt not by chance that the two discoveries that have overturned the cultural world in a span of fifty years belong to what is conventionally called the "human" or "social sciences" and that they break with the *traditional protocols of discovery* in the natural sciences and the theoretical formations of ideology. Nor is it by chance that this common break was experienced by a number of contemporaries, once Marx and Freud become sufficiently well known, as the manifestation of a certain affinity between the two theories. From there, prisoners that they were of the ideological prejudice concerning the "monism" of all scientific objects, it is not by chance that some began to search for the reasons for that affinity in an *identity of object*, such as Reich, seeking to *identify* the effects of the unconscious isolated by Freud with the effects of the class struggle isolated by Marx.

We still live, or in any event, many of us continue to live, with the same intuition: too many things link them together, so *there must be something in common between Marx and Freud*. But what? And if the failed experiment of Reich has showed us where and how *not* to look for their point of encounter (in an identity of object), the conviction persists that something in common is occurring in that double experiment without precedent in the history of culture.

It can be argued in a first instance that in a world equally dominated by idealism and mechanism, Freud, exactly like Marx, offers us the example of a *materialist and dialectical* thought.

If the minimal thesis defining materialism is the existence of reality outside thought or consciousness, Freud is indeed a materialist, since he rejects the primacy of consciousness not only within knowledge but *within consciousness* itself, construing the "psychical apparatus" as a whole of which the ego or the "conscious" is but an agency, part, or effect. At a more general level, Freud's opposition to all idealism, spiritualism, and religion, even when disguised as morality, is well known.

As for dialectic, Freud furnished some surprising manifestations of it, which he never treated as "laws" (that questionable form of a certain Marxist tradition), such as the categories of displacement, condensation, overdetermination, and so on, and also in this limit thesis, whose meditation would take us far: *the unconscious does not know contradiction*; that absence of contradiction is the condition of all contradiction. One finds therein the wherewithal to "shatter" the classical model of contradiction, too intimately inspired by Hegel to serve truly as a "method" for Marxist analysis.

Marx and Freud would thus be close to each other through materialism and dialectic, with a strange advantage accruing to Freud for having explored figures of dialectic very close to those of Marx but also at times richer than them and as though awaited by Marx's theory. If I can quote myself here, I once gave an example of that surprising affinity by showing that the category of *overdetermination* (borrowed from Freud) was as if required and expected by the analyses of Marx and Lenin, to which it was precisely suited, even as it had the advantage of bringing into relief what separated Marx and Lenin from Hegel, for whom contradiction, precisely, *is not overdetermined*.[1]

Are those philosophical affinities sufficient to account for the theoretical community existing between Marx and Freud? Yes and no. We might in fact stop here, for the philosophical yield is already rich, and allow each theory to function on its own, that is, to confront its own object, which *as an object* is irreducible to the philosophical affinities just mentioned; we might, then, withdraw and keep our peace. Yet another phenomenon, which is still more astonishing, should retain our attention, what I have called the *conflictual* character of Marxist theory and Freudian theory.

It is a fact of experience that Freudian theory is a conflictual theory. From its birth—and the phenomenon has not stopped recurring—it provoked not only strong resistance, not only attacks and criticism, but something more interesting, attempts at *annexation* and *revision*. I say that the attempts at annexation and revision are more interesting than simple attacks and criticisms because they indicate that Freudian theory is admitted by its adversaries to contain something *true* and *dangerous*. Where there is no truth, there is no reason to want to annex or revise. There is, then, in Freud something true that has to be appropriated, but in order to revise its meaning, *for that truth is dangerous*: it has to be revised in order to neutralize it. We have there an entire cycle whose dialectic is pitiless, for what is remarkable in this dialectic of resistance-criticism-revision is that the phenomenon, which always begins *outside* Freudian theory (with its adversaries), always ends up *inside* Freudian theory. It is within itself that Freudian theory is obliged to defend itself against attempts at annexation and revision; the adversary always ends up penetrating the fortress, and such is revisionism, provoking internal counterattacks and ending with *scissions*. A *conflictual* science, Freudian theory is a *scissionist* science; its history is marked by endlessly renewed scissions.

Now the idea that a science can be by nature conflictual and scissionist, and subject to a dialectic of resistance-attacks-revision-scissions, is a true scandal for rationalism, even when it declares itself to be materialist. Rationalism has no trouble admitting, if need be, that an entirely new science (Copernicus, Galileo) may come up against the established power of the Church and the prejudices of an "age of ignorance," but it is as if by accident, and only in an initial phase, just enough time for ignorance to be dissipated: *in principle* science, which is reason, always ends up victorious, since "truth is all-powerful" (Lenin himself said, "Marx theory [*la théorie Marx*] is all-powerful because it is true") and stronger than all the shadows in the world. For rationalism, the idea that there might be sciences that are conflictual by nature, haunted or even constituted by contestation and struggle, is pure "nonsense": these are not sciences but simple *opinions*, contradictory in themselves, like all subjective (and consequently disputable) points of view.

Now before Freudian theory Marxist science furnishes us with the example of a necessarily conflictual and scissionist science. This is not an accident or the result of the surprise of ignorance caught short or reigning prejudices challenged in their comfort and their power; it is a matter of a necessity organically linked to the very object of the science founded by Marx. The entire history of Marxist theory and of Marxism proves it, as does first of all, should it be necessary to recall the example, the history of Marx himself. Starting from Hegel and from Feuerbach, in whom he thought he found a critique of Hegel, Marx succeeded in occupying philosophical positions from which he was able to discover his object only through a long internal and external political and philosophical struggle. He succeeded in occupying those positions only on the condition of breaking with the dominant bourgeois ideology, after having politically and intellectually experienced the *antagonistic character* between the world of dominant bourgeois ideology and the political and philosophical positions that allowed him to

discover what the immense edifice of bourgeois ideology and its theoretical formations (philosophy, economics, politics, etc.) had *the mission
of concealing* in order to perpetuate the exploitation and domination of
the bourgeois class. Marx convinced himself in that way that the
"truth" he discovered had as its *accidental* adversary not "error" or
"ignorance" but *the organic system of bourgeois ideology, an essential element
in the bourgeoisie's class struggle.* That "error" had no reason ever to recognize the "truth" (class exploitation) since, on the contrary, its organic class function was to mask it and, in its class struggle, to subject
the exploited to the *system of illusions* indispensable to their submission.
At the very heart of the "truth," Marx encountered the class struggle,
an irreconcilable and merciless struggle. He discovered at the same
time that the science he was founding was a "party science" (Lenin), a
science "representing the proletariat" (*Capital*), thus a science that the
bourgeoisie could never acknowledge but that it would fight to the
death by every means.

The whole history of Marxism has verified, and verifies every day,
the *necessarily conflictual* character of the science founded by Marx.
Marxist theory, "true" and dangerous, quickly became one of the vital
objectives of bourgeois class struggle. One observed the previously
mentioned dialectic come into play: attack-annexation-revision-scis-
sion; one saw the attack coming *from without* pass *into* the theory, which
became invested with revisionism—to which the counterattack of
scission came as a response in certain limit situations (Lenin against the
Second International). It is through that implacable and *inevitable* dialectic of an irreconcilable struggle that Marxist theory grew and
gained strength before traversing grave—and always conflictual—
crises.

These things are known, but one does not always take the measure
of their conditions. It will be admitted that Marxist theory is necessarily enlisted in the class struggle, and that the conflict that pits it against
bourgeois ideology is irremediable, but it will be more difficult to admit that the *conflictuality* of Marxist theory is *constitutive* of its *scientificity*, its *objectivity*. One will retreat to positivist and economist
positions, and the conflictual conditions of the existence of the science
as *contingent* will be distinguished from its scientific results. This
amounts to not seeing that Marxist science and the Marxist investigator are obliged to *take a position* in the conflict whose object is Marxist theory, are obliged to occupy (proletarian) class theoretical posi-

tions, which are opposed to every theoretical position of the bourgeoisie, in order to be able to constitute and develop their science. What are those proletarian class theoretical positions indispensable to the constitution and development of Marxist theory? They are materialist and dialectical *philosophical positions* allowing one to *see* what bourgeois ideology necessarily *conceals*: the class structure and class exploitation of a social formation. Now those philosophical positions are always and necessarily antagonistic to bourgeois positions.

These principles, if not in this formulation (class theoretical positions), at least in their general meaning, are rather broadly recognized by Marxist theorists. Nonetheless one cannot help thinking all too often that they are merely paid lip service, without their profound meaning being assumed and taken into account in all its consequences. Should we attempt to give a less fluent—but perhaps more illuminating—expression of things? There is at the heart of this idea that in order simply to *see* and understand what is transpiring in a class society, it is indispensable to occupy proletarian class theoretical positions, this simple observation that *in a necessarily conflictual reality* like such a society, *one cannot see everything from everywhere*, one can discover the essence of that conflictual reality only on the condition of occupying *certain positions in the conflict itself and not others*, since to occupy passively other positions is to allow oneself to be led into the class illusion known as the dominant ideology. To be sure, that condition runs up against the whole positivist tradition within which bourgeois ideology has interpreted the practice of the sciences of nature, since the condition of positivist objectivity is precisely to occupy a *null* position, *outside of conflict*, whatever it be (once the theological and metaphysical age has passed). But the same condition joins up with another tradition, traces of which may be detected among the greatest figures, such as Machiavelli, who wrote "that one *had to be of the people* in order to *know* Princes." Marx does not say anything else, in substance, in his entire work. When he writes in the preface to *Capital* that that work "*represents* the proletariat," he in effect declares that one has to occupy proletarian positions to know capital. Moreover, if we take Machiavelli's line in its strongest sense and apply it to the history of Marx and his work, it is with some justice that we can say that *one has to be of the proletariat to know capital*. Concretely that means that one has not only to have acknowledged the existence of the proletariat but to have *shared its battles*, as Marx did for four years before the *Manifesto*, to have been a militant in the first organizations of the proletariat in order to be in a position to know capital. To move within the class theoretical positions of the proletariat, there is in effect no other way in the world than *practice*, that is, personal participation in the political struggles of the first forms of proletarian organization. It is through that practice that the intellectual "becomes proletariat," and only if he has "become proletariat," that is, if he has succeeded in displacing himself from bourgeois and petty-bourgeois class theoretical positions to revolutionary theoretical positions, can he "know capital"—as Machiavelli said that "one had to be of the people in order to know Princes." Now *there is no other way for an intellectual "to be of the people" than to become "people" through the practical experience of the struggle of that people.*

Allow me a word here on a too famous formula; it is Kautsky's, and Lenin adopted it in *What Is to Be Done?* It speaks of the fusion of the worker movement and Marxist theory. It says that Marxist theory was elaborated by intellectuals and was introduced *from without* into the workers' movement. I have always been convinced that this formula was unfortunate, for it is quite plain that Marx and Engels were trained as *bourgeois intellectuals* outside the workers' movement: they were trained, like all the intellectuals of their day, in bourgeois universities. Nevertheless Marxist theory has nothing to do with the bourgeois theories with which intellectuals were impregnated; on the contrary, it says something totally alien to the world of bourgeois theory and ideology. How does it happen that highly educated *bourgeois* intellectuals were able to forge and conceive a *revolutionary* theory serving the proletariat by speaking the truth about capital? The answer seems simple to me, and I have already given it in principle: Marx and Engels forged their theory not *outside* the workers' movement but *within* the workers' movement, without ceasing to be intellectuals, not outside the proletariat and its positions but *within* the positions and the revolutionary practice of the proletariat. It is because they had become *organic* intellectuals of the proletariat, and become such through their practice in the workers' movement, that they were able to conceive their theory. That theory was not "imported from without" into the workers' movement; it was conceived through an immense theoretical effort *inside* the workers' movement. The pseudo-*importation* mentioned by Kautsky is but the *expansion*, within the workers' movement, of a theory produced *within* the workers' movement by organic intellectuals of the proletariat.

At stake here are not subsidiary questions relating to details or curiosity but problems that involve the meaning of the entirety of Marx's work. For that "displacement" (which Freud so liked to speak about on the subject of his object) onto revolutionary class theoretical positions does not have, as one might think, merely political consequences. Concretely the political-theoretical or philosophical act of abandoning bourgeois or petty-bourgeois theoretical positions to arrive at proletarian class theoretical positions is laden with theoretical and scientific consequences. It is not by chance that Marx wrote, as a subtitle for *Capital*, this simple formula:"*Critique of Political Economy*." Nor is it by chance that the meaning of the "critique" has so often been misunderstood as a *judgment* by Marx on an undisputed and indisputable reality, reducing it to debates as to whether Smith and Ricardo did indeed understand this or that, did see surplus value behind income or not, and so on. Things go infinitely further. In the "displacement" that has him occupying proletarian class theoretical positions, Marx discovers that despite all the merits of its authors, political economy as it exists is not fundamentally a *science* but a *theoretical formation of bourgeois ideology*, playing its role in the ideological class struggle. He discovers that it is not only the detail of existing political economy that is to be criticized but that the very idea, the project, and thus the existence of *political economy*—which can be thought of as an independent and autonomous discipline only on the condition of disguising class relations and the class struggle that it is its ideological mission to conceal—deserve to be called into question and doubt. Marx's theoretical revolution thus arrives at the conclusion *that there is no political economy* (except for the bourgeoisie, whose interests are all too clear) and that it is all the more emphatically the case that *there is no Marxist political economy*. That does not mean that there is nothing; rather, it means that Marx replaces the object that political economy was alleged to be with *an entirely different reality* that becomes intelligible through *entirely different principles*, those of historical materialism, *in which class struggle becomes determinant for understanding so-called economic phenomena*.

One might multiply examples in Marx, showing that his theory of class struggle is completely different from the bourgeois theory or that his theory of ideology and the state is equally disconcerting. In every case one can establish a relation between the displacement onto class theoretical positions and the revolution in the object (which becomes wholly other, undergoing a change not merely in its limits but in its nature and *identity*) and the practico-revolutionary consequences. It is certain that this major change in traditional protocols of recognition has not facilitated the task of Marx's readers. What has jolted them more than anything else, however, is the scientific and theoretical fertility of a conflictual science.

Granted, it will be said, but what of Freud in all this? Now it happens that, with all due proportion and at a different level, Freudian theory is in an analogous situation with respect to *conflictuality*.

In elaborating his theory of the unconscious, Freud in fact touched on an extraordinarily sensitive point of philosophical, psychological, and moral ideology, calling into question, through the discovery of the unconscious and its effects, a certain "natural" and "spontaneous" idea of "man" as a "*subject*" whose *unity* is *ensured* or *crowned* by "*consciousness.*"

It happens as well that this ideology has a hard time renouncing that key conception without renouncing its role. It (its "functionaries," Marx said) resists, criticizes, attacks, and in turn attempts to infiltrate Freudian theory, to revise it from within after having attacked it from without. We recognize there the dialectic that we already analyzed— the one that grounds the necessarily conflictual character of Freudian theory.

But, it will be said, what common denominator allows one to compare the hostility of that bourgeois ideology of man toward the theory of the unconscious to the hostility of bourgeois ideology toward the theory of class struggle? Is not what is necessary in the case of Marx relatively contingent in that of Freud? How can one compare what is valid for the class struggle of a society with the defensive reflex of an ideology of man?

In point of fact, the comparison is not as arbitrary as it might appear. The ideology of man as a subject whose *unity* is ensured or crowned by consciousness is not just any fragmentary ideology; it is quite simply *the philosophical form of bourgeois ideology* that has dominated history for five centuries and that, even if it today no longer has its former vigor, still reigns over large sectors of idealist philosophy and constitutes the implicit philosophy of psychology, morality, and even political economy. It is not useful at this juncture to recall that the great idealist tradition of bourgeois philosophy was a *philosophy of "consciousness,"* be it empirical or transcendental, since everyone knows it, even if that tradition is in the process of giving way to neopositivism. It is, on the other hand, more important to recall that this ideology of the *conscious subject* constituted the implicit philosophy of classical political economy and that Marx was criticizing its "economic" version in rejecting any idea of "*homo economicus*," in which man is defined as the conscious subject of his needs and that subject of need is defined as the ultimate and constitutive element of every society. With that Marx rejected the idea that one could find in man as subject of his needs not only the ultimate explanation of society but also, *and this is crucial, the explanation of man as subject*, that is, as a self-identical and self-identifiable unity, one identifiable in particular by that "self" par excellence which is self-consciousness. The golden rule of materialism is *do not judge being by its self-consciousness*, for every being is other than its self-consciousness. But it is perhaps still more important to point out that the philosophical category of the self-conscious subject finds its natural embodiment *in the bourgeois conception of morality and psychology*. One understands that morality needs a self-conscious subject, one responsible for its deeds, so that one can oblige it "in conscience" to obey norms that it is more "economical" not to impose on it through violence. One understands, moreover, by the simple definition of the moral subject (or subject of its deeds) that this subject is but *the necessary complement of the subject of law*, who must indeed be a subject and conscious to have an *identity* and account for what it owes as a function of the laws of which it is "alleged not to be ignorant," a subject who is to be aware of the laws constraining it (Kant), but without obliging it "in conscience." It will thus be suspected that the famous "*psychological subject*," which in all cases was and remains the object of a "science" (psychology), is not a crude and natural given but a strange and problematic hybrid caught up in the philosophical fate of all the "subjects" haunting it: subject of law, subject of needs, moral (and religious) subject, political subject, and so on.

It would be easy, if we had enough time at our disposal, to show the ideological conspiracy forged (under the dominance of bourgeois ideology) around the notion of the "*self-conscious subject*," a *highly problematic* "reality" for any possible or impossible science of man but, on the other hand, a reality terrifically needed by the structure of a class society. In the category of the self-conscious subject, bourgeois ideology *represents* to individuals what they *ought* to be in order to accept their own submission to bourgeois ideology; it represents them as endowed with the *unity* and the *consciousness* (that very unity) they ought to have in order to unify their different practices and different deeds under the unity of the dominant ideology.

I am deliberately insisting on the category of *unity* inseparable from all *consciousness*. It is not an accident if the entire bourgeois philosophical tradition presents consciousness as the faculty of unification, the faculty of synthesis, be it in the framework of the empiricism of Locke or Hume or in that of a transcendental philosophy that, after long obsessing his precursors, found expression in Kant. That consciousness is *synthesis* means that it realizes within the subject the unity of the diversity of its sense impressions (from perception to knowledge), the unity of its moral acts, and the unity of its religious aspirations, as it does the unity of its political practices. Consciousness thus appears as the *function* (delegated to the individual by the "nature of man") of *unification* of the diversity of its practices, be they cognitive, moral, or political. Let's translate this abstract language: *consciousness is obligatory* for the individual endowed with it to realize in himself the *unity* required by bourgeois ideology, so that subjects conform to its own ideological and political imperative of *unity*, in brief, for *the conflictual rift of the class struggle to be lived by its agents as a superior and "spiritual" form of unity*. I am deliberately insisting on this *unity*, in other words, on the identity of *consciousness and the function of unity*, because it was there that Marx's critique came forcefully to bear when he *dismantled the illusory unity* of bourgeois ideology and the phantasm of unity it produces within *consciousness* as the effect it needs to function. I am deliberately insisting on this *unity* because, through an encounter charged with meaning, it was there that the Freudian critique of consciousness came to focus.

In truth, if one understands Marx well, there is no mystery pertaining to the "sensitive point" Freud wounded within the whole classical philosophical tradition, as well as in the *theoretical* formations of bourgeois ideology, such as psychology, sociology, and political economy, or in *practical* formations such as morality and religion. It is enough to understand that the various "conscious subjects of" are *unifiers of the social identity of the individual insofar as they are unified as so many exemplars of an ideology of "man,"* a being "naturally endowed with consciousness," to apprehend the profound unity of that ideology and its theoretical and practical formations. It is enough to grasp that profound unity to perceive the reasons for the depth of the resistance to Freud. In discovering the unconscious, that reality he did not expect, in what we may call his political innocence, which concealed a strong ideological sensibility, Freud did not touch on only *one* "sensitive point" of existing philosophical, moral, and psychological ideology; he did not unsettle ideas that happened to be there by chance, as a result of the development of knowledge or human illusion; he did not touch on a sensitive but secondary point of a local random ideology. Perhaps without knowing it during the first years (but he realized it very quickly), he touched on theoretically *the most sensitive* point of the entire system of bourgeois ideology. The paradox is that Freud, with the exception of a few random and debatable essays (*Totem and Taboo, Civilization and Its Discontents*, etc.), never truly attempted to embrace as a whole that bourgeois ideology that he was unsettling at its most sensitive point. Let us go further: he was in no position to do so, for to do that he would have to have been Marx. He was not Marx; he had *an entirely different object*. Nevertheless it was enough that he revealed to a dumbfounded world that *this other object* existed for the consequences to be drawn by themselves and for the uninterrupted attacks of all those who (for one reason or another, but because they were united in the conviction of the dominant ideology) had an interest *in his remaining silent* to be launched against him. Freud's line on approaching America when he visited there is well known: "we're bringing them the plague." One thinks of Marx's line speaking of *Capital* as "the most gigantic missile launched at the head of the capitalist bourgeoisie." These are the words of men who not only knew what it means to fight but who also knew that they were bringing into the world sciences that could exist only in and through struggle, since the adversary could not tolerate their existence: conflictual sciences, with no compromise possible.

One should not be content with these generalities, however, no matter how accurate they are, for this simple reason: *Freud's object is not Marx's object.* There was, in fact, in Freud something quite idiosyncratic, which results in the comparison simultaneously stopping short and rebounding anew.

Freud's object is not Marx's object. Marx asks himself what a social formation is and recognizes in it the determining role of class struggle, from which he elaborates his entire theory of the relation between relations of production and productive forces and his theory of superstructure (law and state, ideology). The requisite theoretical condition governing this theory, in which *relations* (of production, of class, etc.) are determinant and the idea of a *causality by relations* and not by elements is presupposed, is to reject the theoretical presupposition of classical political economy or idealist theories of history, namely, that it is *individuals* who are *the* (originary) *subjects* (as ultimate causes) of the entire economic or historical process. That is why Marx takes care on numerous occasions in *Capital* to specify that individuals must be considered as *supports* (*Träger*) of *functions*, those functions being themselves determined and fixed by (economic, political, ideological) *relations* of class struggle that move the entire social structure, even when it does no more than reproduce itself. In the introduction to the *Contribution* Marx says that one must start out not from the "concrete but from the abstract." That theory of the primacy of relations over terms, that theory of (capitalist or proletarian) individuals as "supports of functions," confirms the thesis of the introduction. It is not that Marx ever loses sight of concrete individuals, but since they are also "concrete," they are "the synthesis of numerous determinations," and to discover the laws of capitalist society, in which those individuals exist, live, and fight, *Capital* restricts itself to the study of the most important of those numerous determinations, without proposing to reconstitute through "the synthesis of numerous determinations" the concrete individuals, whom it provisionally considers only in relation to their role as supports. In any event, *Capital* tells us enough, and Marx's historical texts are sufficiently explicit for us to know that *Marx was unable to go beyond a theory of social individuality or historical forms of individuality.* There is nothing in Marx that anticipates Freud's discovery; *there is nothing in Marx that can ground a theory of the psyche.*

In those essays of unfortunate generalization, however, Freud in fact did not stop *repeating* in questionable conditions what he had discovered *elsewhere.* Now what he had discovered bore in no way on "society" or "social relations" but on very particular phenomena affecting *individuals.* Although it has been possible to maintain that there is a "transindividual" element in the unconscious, it is in any event *within the individual* that the effects of the unconscious become manifest, and it is *on the individual* that therapy operates, even if it requires the presence of another individual (the analyst) to transform the existing effects of the unconscious. That difference suffices to distinguish Freud from Marx.

It distinguishes them even if one can find strange resemblances in the respective conditions of their discovery. I insisted a few moments ago on the fact that the intellectual must "become of the people" to understand princes; I even allowed it to be understood that the transformation that causes him to move from bourgeois and petty-bourgeois class theoretical positions to proletarian positions, solely on the basis of which it is possible to *see* exploitation and class struggle, occur by way of political practice. One can even go a bit further and say that an intellectual can become an organic intellectual of the proletariat *only if he is educated* by the class struggle of the proletariat, which transforms his previous positions and allows him to *see*. It has been possible to maintain, with strong arguments in support, that something analogous occurred with Freud: if he changed his position with respect to the problems of consciousness, if he broke with physiology and medicine, it was *because he was educated by his own hysterical patients,* who literally *taught* him and *allowed him to see* that there existed a language of the unconscious inscribed in their bodies, and it was Anna O. who not only invented the term "talking cure" for him (a decisive stage in the discovery) but imposed on him a recognition of the existence of transference and countertransference. There is in this a gripping aspect of the history of psychoanalysis that materialists would do well to ponder.[2]

It remains that at first sight, what Freud discovered occurs in the individual. It is here that we reencounter an unexpected form of conflictuality, and with it a new difference between Freud and Marx, and at the same time a principle that no doubt enters in part in the effect of subjection exercised by ideology over its "subjects." It appears in fact that the massive refusal of psychoanalysis by philosophers (or the "revision" they subject it to in order to destroy its ambitions)—including Marxist materialists, who too often take refuge in an "ontological" conception of the Leninist thesis of consciousness as reflection—physicians, psychologists, moralists, and others *is not due solely* to a mass ideological antagonism, even if this antagonism is inevitable at the mass level. It seems that another specific determination must be added to that antagonism to explain its specific "allure": the fact that it is "propped" on a characteristic of the unconscious object itself. That supplementary element pertains to the "nature" of the unconscious, which is *repression*. If such be the case, it does not seem risky to posit that individuals resist the idea of the unconscious not for reasons of an exclusively ideological character but . . . *because they themselves have an unconscious* that automatically represses, in a repetition compulsion (*Wiederholungszwang*), the idea of the existence of the unconscious. Every individual thus "spontaneously" develops a reflex of "defense" when confronting the unconscious, which is part of his own unconscious, a *repression* of the possibility of the unconscious, which coincides with the unconscious itself. Every individual? This is not certain. It is not established that the defensive reflex is always equally active; experience shows, on the contrary, that there exist subjects in whom that resistance is—by virtue of the accommodation of their phantasmatic conflicts—sufficiently superseded to permit them to acknowledge the reality of the unconscious without triggering a reflex of defense or flight.

But by this path, as by others, we enter into Freud's discovery. What did Freud discover? I will not be expected to furnish a presentation of Freudian theory, but the following few remarks *situate* it theoretically.

It would be an absurdity to believe that Freud proposed—like the behaviorists, whose attempt he mocked—the idea of a *psychology without consciousness*. Quite to the contrary, he accords its place to "the fundamental fact of consciousness" in the psychical apparatus, attributes to it a special "system" ("perception-consciousness") at the limit of the outside world and a privileged role in therapy. In addition he affirms that there is no unconscious possible except in a conscious being. Nonetheless, concerning the ideological primacy of consciousness, Freud is pitiless: "we must learn to *emancipate* ourselves from the importance attributed to the symptom of "being conscious." Why? Because consciousness is incapable on its own of furnishing a "distinction *between systems.*"

Freud in fact not only discovered the existence of the unconscious; he also maintained that the psychical is structured [not] on the model of a *unity centered* on consciousness but as an "apparatus" containing "different systems" irreducible to a *unique* principle. In the first topographical model (spatial figuration) this apparatus contains the unconscious, the preconscious, and the conscious, with the agency of a "censor" repressing into the unconscious representations of drives that are unbearable for the preconscious and the conscious. In the second topographical model the apparatus consists of the id, the ego, and the superego, repression being the responsibility of a part of the ego and the superego.

This apparatus is not a *centered unity* but a complex of agencies constituted by the play of unconscious repression. The shattering of the subject, the decentering of the psychical apparatus in relation to the conscious and the ego, is accompanied by a revolutionary theory of the ego: the ego, formerly the sole seat of consciousness, itself becomes in large part unconscious, fully participant in the conflict of unconscious repression in which the agencies are constituted. That is why consciousness is blind to the "difference of the system*s*," in which it is but *one* system among others, whose totality is subject to the *conflictual dynamic* of repression.

To be sure, one cannot help thinking, at a distance, of the revolution introduced by Marx when he abandoned the bourgeois ideological myth that thought the nature of society as a *unified* and *centered whole* in order to think every social formation as a system of instances *without center*. Freud, who almost did not know Marx, like him thought his object (although it had nothing in common with Marx's) within the spatial figuration of a "topographical model" (think of the preface to the 1859 *Contribution*) and of a *topographical model without center*, in which the various instances have no unity other than *the unity of their conflictual functioning*, in what Freud calls "the psychical apparatus," a term (apparatus) that seems no less discreetly allusive to Marx.

I mention these theoretical affinities between Marx and Freud to communicate the extent to which this major change in traditional *forms of thought* and the introduction of revolutionary forms of thought (topography, apparatus, conflictual instances without any center and possessing as their only unity that of their conflictual functioning, the necessary illusion of the identity of the ego, etc.) could either indicate the presence of a bewildering object, the unconscious, or come up against the ideology it forbade and the repression it aroused.

From that point one can attempt to define negatively the position of the Freudian unconscious.

The Freudian unconscious is *psychical*, which excludes identifying it, as an entire mechanical-materialist tendency would be inclined to, with the *nonpsychical* or with an effect derived from the nonpsychical. The Freudian unconscious, in this respect, is neither a material reality (the body, the brain, the "biological," the "psychophysiological") nor a social reality (the social relations defined by Marx as determining individuals *independently of their consciousness*), different from "consciousness," and thus from the psyche, but producing or determining consciousness unwittingly. Not that Freud ever denied the existence of a relation between the unconscious, on the one hand, and the biological and the social, on the other. All psychical life is "propped" on the

biological by way of drives, which Freud conceives as "representations" sent by the somatic into the psychical. Through this concept of
representation Freud acquits himself of his objective recognition of the
biological anchoring of the drive (which is always sexual, at bottom),
but through that same concept he frees the drive of unconscious desire from any *essential determination* by the biological: the drive is a "*limit
concept between the somatic and the psychical*"; it is at the same time the
concept of that limit, that is, of the *difference* between the somatic and
the psychical. Nor did Freud ever deny the existence of a relation between the system of instances or agencies of the ego and objective or
social reality, whose trace is found not only in the "reality principle"
but also in the perception-consciousness system and in the superego.
There too, however, in his insistence on speaking of an "external surface" of the psychical apparatus, Freud is again thinking a *limit*: the
propping on the external and social world simultaneously designates a
difference of reality, its acknowledgment, and its identification.

No doubt that for Freud the phenomena produced by the psychical apparatus, and above all effects of the unconscious, constitute a veritable reality, but a reality sui generis: "Should we recognize a reality in
unconscious wishes? I am incapable of saying. . . . When one confronts
unconscious wishes reduced to their ultimate and truest expression,
*one is indeed forced to say that psychical reality is a particular form of existence,
which should not be confused with material reality*." Or again: "For unconscious processes (objective, material) *reality* testing has no impact;
thought reality is equivalent to external reality; wishes are equivalent
to their fulfillment. . . . One should never err by transporting *the value
of reality* into repressed psychical formations. . . . One is obliged to use
the currency reigning in the country one is exploring" ("On the Two
Principles of Psychical Activity").

If it designates that reality sui generis, unique unto itself, the
Freudian unconscious clearly has nothing to do with the unconscious
of the philosophical tradition: Platonic forgetting, the indiscernible in
Leibniz, and even the "back" of Hegelian self-consciousness. That unconscious is always an accident or a modality of *consciousness*, consciousness of truth "overlayed" with a corporeal forgetting but subsist-
ing in itself despite that forgetting (Plato), the infinitesimal aspect of a
consciousness too "small" to be "perceived" (Leibniz), or consciousness present in itself in the in-itself/for-itself of self-consciousness before discovering itself in the new for-itself of self-consciousness

(Hegel). That entire philosophical tradition regards consciousness as *the "truth"* of its unconscious forms, that is, regards the unconscious as simply *consciousness misconstrued.* The fate of philosophy is to "remove" that misperception for truth to be "unveiled." To take things from this symptomatic and limited angle, one might say that in Freud consciousness is never the "truth" of its unconscious forms, first because the relation of consciousness to unconscious forms is not a relation of *property* ("its" forms), which can be put as follows: consciousness is not the subject of the unconscious—a thesis that can be verified in therapy, in which, whatever has been claimed, it is a matter not of consciousness reappropriating "its truth" in the currency of its unconscious but of contributing to a restructuring of the array of phantasms in an unconscious that is subject to the labor (*Durcharbeit*) of analysis.

In concluding, I would like to insist on a final point. The Freudian unconscious is not a *nonconscious* psychical structure that psychology would reconstitute on the basis of stereotypes or the general demeanor of an individual's behavior, as their so-called unconscious premontage. In France we have known an interpretation of this type in Merleau-Ponty, who "read" Freud in the dual light of behaviorist psychology and Husserl's philosophy of the transcendental concrete. Merleau-Ponty had a tendency to think of that "structure of behavior" as a *prepredicative* a priori determining the meaning and style of behavior *somewhere beneath* individuals' thetic consciousness. He sought in the categories of synthesis and prepredicative structure a way of joining up with the Freudian unconscious. Theories of the same nature can be developed without resorting explicitly to Husserl, but they can hardly do without a psychology of behavior or, more subtly, the psychology of P. Janet, even when based on a "materialist" genesis of the stereotypes of structures of behavior.

I believe that one can address two criticisms to this attempt from the Freudian point of view. The first is that this theory of the unconscious as a "montage" of behavioral patterns does not call into question what is, as we have seen, at the heart of psychological ideology: the *unity* of the *subject* considered as the subject of *his* behavior and *his* acts (the fact that one can ultimately exclude consciousness does not affect this principle of *unity*). The second is that this attempt does not "shift ground" in relation to that of psychology; it *duplicates,* in the form of "reality" it calls "unconscious," the structure of patterns of behavior, whether conscious or not. It matters little whether this duplication is transcendental or empirical (and genetic); what it attains resembles the *nonconscious* we have mentioned rather than the Freudian unconscious. One should not mistake unconsciouses. Remember Freud's line: "One is obliged to use the currency reigning in the country one is exploring" and no other.

4

"In the Name of the Analysands . . ."

1980

On Monday, March 17, 1980, the day after the famous meeting of the Ecole Freudienne de Paris (EFP) organized at the Hotel PLM Saint-Jacques following Jacques Lacan's decision to "dissolve" his school—against the advice of a portion of its members—Catherine Clément related the event in Le Matin *under the title "Louis Althusser Attacks the Lacan Fortress." She was in fact relying essentially on the* "Lettre ouverte aux analysands et analystes se réclamant de Jacques Lacan" *(Open letter to analysands and analysts in solidarity with Jacques Lacan), which was written by Louis Althusser the day after the meeting, at the request, he wrote, of Jacques-Alain Miller—his former student at the Ecole Normale and one of the active participants in his 1963–1964 seminar on psychoanalysis—and to be published in the "temporary bulletin" of the Ecole Freudienne entitled* Delenda. *That publication would not take place.[1]*

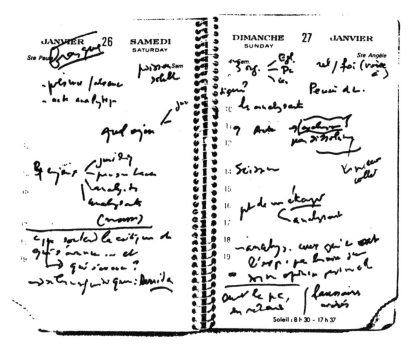

Facsimile of two pages from Louis Althusser's appointment book on which he had "jotted down a few notes" for his intervention at the meeting of the PLM-Saint-Jacques, March 15, 1980. (Althusser Archives/IMEC.)

In that "open letter," published here, Louis Althusser related his untimely outburst at that assembly and the spectacular and violent intervention he subsequently made in the presence of Lacan, whom he characterized as a "magnificent and pitiful Harlequin." We reproduce in facsimile the two pages of his notebook on which he had set down the principal themes of his largely improvised intervention.

Following the article in Le Matin, Louis Althusser, shocked by its title, which he judged to be "sensationalistic and mendacious," took up anew and expanded his analysis of the event. Only the first eleven typed pages of that second text have been found; it was quite probably abandoned before completion. They figure among the last pages written by Althusser on Lacan and psychoanalysis, with the exception, to be sure, of what he would subsequently furnish in The Future Lasts Forever, *evoking that last encounter with Lacan.[2]*

Open Letter to Analysands and Analysts in Solidarity with Jacques Lacan

J.-A. Miller asked me yesterday whether I was willing to write a few words for this temporary bulletin. Of course I am. Exactly as, although uninvited, I introduced myself last night around 6:20 into the great hall of the PLM, where Lacan, standing, his head bent over a text that may not have existed under his eyes, spoke in a sad and fatigued half-voice before 500 apparently fascinated persons, exactly as, questioned last night by a young woman who was "filtering at the entrance" and who had imprudently allowed me to pass without saying anything, I replied to her question, "Have you been invited?" with "Yes: by the Holy Ghost, and not by God the Father, but that's even better," since I re-called having explained the previous evening, before a marvelous friend who is a philosopher, a theologian sui generis, and a painter (who is occasionally excellent, when he doesn't follow the advice of the owner of his gallery), that the Holy Ghost is quite simply libido, something one does not know, and that ever since it has been known, one doesn't give a damn for the Holy Ghost any more than for God; Christ is something else because he was a man, one who existed, spoke, and acted by chasing the merchants out of the temple and by inaugu-rating a "new practice of philosophy," which is of the greatest interest to us and which is to "forgive one's enemies" (note the "forgive," which has aged terrifically, thank God, Spinoza and Nietzsche and Lenin and Mao passed by there). And so I listened, from the back of the room where J.-A. Miller, an old acquaintance from the Ecole, had taken me, and after a certain number of minutes I began to read *Le Monde*, so much did all I was able to hear (with difficulty from the mouth of the "master," that unfortunate and pitiful Harlequin of eighty years, dressed in a magnificent tweed jacket patterned with blue diamond shapes) depress me, appall me, and so on, including, to be sure, if one say, Lacan. Nothing new to "pinpoint" in his monotone lecture, delivered more for his own use—might he need, then, to create still another religion for himself?—than for that of his audience. He spoke simply, a few puns here and there to indicate that it was he, that he was still the same and able to bug the hell out of people, but without any histrionics—in brief, some scratches from a big blue-diamond cat to show that he wasn't sleeping but could still claw and put on a show.

There followed a silence of five whole minutes, then those whom Lacan had, on his own authority, called to the podium started to try to relate (briefly and in very clear, simple, modest language, which proves, all the same, that there is hope, since an individual's way of speaking is laden with meaning and destiny) their mood—there's no other word for it—and on the subject of what? It is more or less impossible to say, at least for all. There was a woman to say (from the podium), "Gotta know what we're gonna do tomorrow" (an assembly to decide on the provisional injunction demanded by certain members of the EFP, in fact to vote for or against the dissolution of the EFP, which Lacan decided on without consulting anyone, knowing all the while, I think, that his decision was a political act [not of dissolution but of exclusion disguised as dissolution], thus had nothing to do with analysis [we'll come back to this] and would automatically provoke a court procedure). The others spoke of their dumbfoundedness, their anger, their humility; in sum, the whole of the *Traité des Passions* could have been pressed into service, but it's already been done, and a lot better, quite a few years ago.

Following the people seated behind the pulpit, others spoke from the floor, but with intervals of singular silences that became—but only after a good hour—increasingly brief, since a certain nervousness was beginning to settle over some. Always two themes: affective reactions to Lacan's decision (enthusiasm, dumbfoundedness, warm agreement, a will to convince . . .)—Lacan still keeping his peace in his blue silence crowned by a fine gray-white haircut—and tomorrow's business, Sunday, March 16, where there would have to be a vote in the plenary session of the EFP, called according to regulations as demanded by law, Lacan, however great he be, not having the power to dissolve on his own say-so an association of 1901. Very vaguely an intervention, two or three, letting it be understood, but implicitly: maybe one had to know what was going to happen and what one wanted. To which those who know (J.-A. Miller, etc.) responded that the dissolution was not simply juridical, that what was needed, as far as mourning was concerned, was a whole "labor" (dissolution work), that it was thus "internal" and to be pursued infinitely until one could not go further or burst in the process. But dissolve what? With their infantile genius for intentional puns (not slips of the tongue, *nota bene*) some said, we've got to dissolve "*la colle de l'Ecole*"[1] [the glue of the Ecole], because we have all flunked [*on est tous collés*], and to dissolve the glue [*la colle*], we have got to dissolve the Ecole. But not one asked whether in dissolving the Ecole and founding "la Cause Freudienne," Lacan was not dragging them into a new Ecole. No. Were you to ask that simple question, you would have been, as happened to me on another matter, crudely put in your place.[2]

Things lasted like that until 10:30, when the glasses were waiting with vodka and everything you could want on the side. Then some other things happened. Before speaking about them, however, I have to recount the sequence of these insignificant events.

It was an old friend, an analyst, who had asked me to come: "Now's the moment or never; come help us," meaning himself and a few others. But he and the few others (in fact, many others, I perceived) promptly lost their courage, didn't peep a word; I was seated at the back of the room alongside J.-A. Miller, and I told him, "all the same, it's unbearable to hear interventions of such a feeble level (it was as though a woman were patiently sorting out beans in her kitchen, on a plate, while a general war and storm were unleashed on the world: deaf!). Why are you silent?" And he: "I'm waiting because one has to let people express themselves; they have interesting things to say." So be it. I gave myself three-quarters of an hour of forced patience, and then I went to see my friends who had asked me to come and asked them this question: "But what are you waiting for?" There was no answer except for an incomprehensible evasion. "But would you be afraid? Of what? Of Lacan? Of yourselves? Of the idea of being an analyst?" And so on. Total silence. I then said to myself that this is no longer bearable, and saying that I needed a table on which to rest my notebook, in which I had jotted down some notes, I climbed up to the podium, shook hands with a silent Lacan (I wondered whether he would consent to extend his hand to me; he waited nearly six seconds—that counts—offering a freckled hand in which there circulated only lassitude, or perhaps old age, that disgrace). I mount the podium, take a mike, and there, before people all of whom don't know me, I say why, although uninvited, I am there, that I am "self-authorized" by virtue of the old acquaintance and friendship I have with Lacan and for him, and I have things to say.

I proceed gently, I say only that there is in this meeting for which there is no agenda (strange!), in this meeting where people are arguing about questions of juridical procedure (tomorrow) that might have been resolved in two minutes if those in charge had not shown themselves to be so irresponsible, that is, if they had consented to furnish everyone, on entering, with a typed page containing the necessary information as to the stage (and this is elementary in its simplicity) that the judicial procedure had reached. I say that despite the absence of an agenda, the meeting had certain issues at stake, and I enumerate them: (1) the judicial issue of the meeting the next day, March 16 (knowing whether to vote yes or no on dissolution); (2) the issue of Lacan's thought, whether it holds up (and I say that it is a crucial question and that no one made the slightest allusion to it); (3) the issue of the analysts that you are; and finally (4) the issue of issues, the heart and the hell of issues, the existence of hundreds of thousands of analysands, and perhaps millions of analysands, who are in analysis with analysts claiming solidarity with the person or the thought of Lacan, and that is the responsibility of responsibilities, or the irresponsibility of irresponsibilities, since ultimately, there is no need to cite cases that everybody has in mind; it is a question of death, of survival, rebirth, transformation, or suicide. There too everyone kept an opaque silence; one would think that you had eradicated your analysands from your list of worries, perhaps only this evening or always, so why receive them and listen to them? All the same, not for the cash, is it? So why this silence? The answer would have to be torn from them, but in private, since publicly it would be impossible, you bet! For those who were speaking face-to-face, either from the neighboring seat or later on in front of a scotch, when they manage it, there is a single answer for everyone—"fear"—and once again, if you ask of whom, you get the range of answers indicated before.

I went no further; there was a pause of a half-hour during which I spoke to some analysts I didn't know; one of them made a recording. It is interesting, I told them, but go drum up some people and let the meeting continue, for I feel like arguing with you in order to see things more clearly. No. They didn't move; they didn't want to. Why? This time whom did they fear? Me? I was flattered, but no thanks.

There then took place a second meeting, for the next day and for the bulletin. For the next day, the same circus started up again. Technical specifications were given for the bulletin. Then some new expressions of mood, whereupon I again intervened, quite calm, but all the same, I was fed up. The most surprising of all in that meeting, which was "feeble" (I quote an analyst who was there and whom I don't know, but she, too, refused to say in public what she thought) and literally infantile (people had no idea of what law, jurisprudence, justice, and legal procedure are and thus of what they would be forced to confront the following day and of the margin of choice offered them; J.-A. Miller, who with the indefatigable patience of a lay monk [something I admired] calmly preaching to the crowds while waiting for the Holy Ghost to have the time and the inclination to descend on them, had to explain the thing in detail)—the most surprising of all, then, in that feeble-infantile meeting, was not that it was so; it was that the people who were there, taken individually (at least those with whom, by pure chance, I spoke) were good people, with ideas that were often—not always—critical of Lacan, but *not one was willing to open up* in public. I asked, "But why?" They answered, "Fear." I asked, "But if you are afraid, why come?" Answer: "It must be that we feel like being afraid." Okay, then, but fear of whom? Answer: see above: fear of Lacan above all (but he had said, "everyone loves me"), afraid of . . . so it's a way of loving, granted, but is it the best, the right one, or the worst, and if it were a way of hating, or of loving oneself (then staying home would settle matters) or a way of bearing-oneself-not-bearing-oneself, or a well-camouflaged way of being out of place (for it is not enough to want to be afraid to be so; you know and are acquainted with the line of Lacan and Ey on the madman: wanting to be mad won't make you so). At that extreme, one can depend on silence.

So I intervened in the course of the second meeting (while leaving the first I got myself insulted by a man who had violently asked me what right I had to go into an auditorium without being invited; I simply answered him, "What kind of inspector are you: train conductor, general inspector of a bank or administration, PCF commissioner, the Holy Office, or the police?"). I intervened to say that this story of the dissolving of the EFP was not my business, but from listening to you, there is a juridical procedure that Lacan has clearly started, whether he wants it or not, and he must know it, for he knows the law, and the whole business is simple: knowing whether one should vote yes or no tomorrow on the subject of dissolution. On that I have no opinion, but it is a political act, and such an act is not taken alone, as Lacan did, but should be reflected on and discussed democratically by all the interested parties, in the first rank of which are your "masses," who are the analysands, your "masses" and your "real teachers" which the analysands are, and not by a single individual in the secrecy of 5 rue de Lille; otherwise, it's despotism, even if it's enlightened. I told them that the juridical affair was a trifle; two minutes are enough to resolve it, and let's move on to serious matters, and, to summarize it all, I have a question to ask you, a single one, which is, "What do you want? You mean that you want what Lacan wants, for the most part, the majority of you? Granted. But do you know what Lacan wants? Do you know whether he might by chance not want anything at all? After all, he's eighty years old, and he has a right to rest, to strawberries, a cameo jacket, silence, to not want anything and to bug the hell out of you and mystify you into the bargain—and what if putting you on gave the man his desired relaxation? But you, what do you want on your own behalf?" Concerning that series of urgent questions, everyone, keeping their peace, could observe that all answered with the most opaque of silences (that is, the most transparent, see my previous remarks).

I note merely that J.-A. Miller saw it fitting, since I had evoked my experience of two organizations other than the one whose meeting I was attending, namely, the Catholic church and the French Communist party, to say that I was poorly placed "to give lessons" (*sic!!!*) given that after my articles in *Le Monde*,[3] which showed "a certain sense of freedom," I had in the end quite simply reentered the ranks and that the "effects of my intervention had been null, totally null." To which I satisfied myself by replying, otherwise J.-A. Miller would have been publicly humiliated at having so crudely and insultingly advanced on terrain he has absolutely no knowledge of, that "this was a personal matter" (you bet!) and that I would not respond in public.

There remains a final observation that is absolutely crucial and that infinitely transcends Lacan and all his thought. It transcends it precisely because Lacan's thought, whatever he may think, does not escape this absolutely mind-boggling phenomenon I am about to relate. The whole meeting was dominated from one end to the other, without the slightest effort at criticism regarding this point, by a profound conviction (I am speaking, of course, of those who spoke and not of the others, who thought no less of it; the words that people utter, however, even if they don't think what they mean—one has to believe all the same that it's not for nothing that they talk and that even should they fail to say it, at least they have something to say), by a *conviction* broadly and constantly evoked, invoked, developed, and augmented, to wit: *a conviction that what was going on in the meeting was part of analysis.* It began when one of the first speakers on the podium said that the decision was "an analytic act" and they all more or less took up the same theme, extending it to all sorts of comparisons, including the session they were experiencing; they thought of the meeting in analytic terms, in terms of a therapeutic session, and of Lacan's act as an "analytic act" (I know what a medical act is, given the legal definition, but an analytic act …). Whatever the case, I told them, in point of fact, you are doing politics and nothing else; you are in the process of doing politics and nothing else, and why do you need to tell yourselves and to tell us this garbage that what Lacan accomplished, what you are in the process of accomplishing, is, for Lacan, the so-called psychoanalytic act of dissolving the Ecole Freudienne and, for you, the psychoanalytic act of palming off your signature to him at the bottom of your moods and of being here tonight shutting up, while hoping no doubt from the silence in which you maintain yourselves and from the words emanating from the mouth of our holy man (or from [his] silence) for the wherewithal to understand what you are doing and what [you] want. But that's rubbish! So long as you insist on imposing at whatever cost on others and on yourselves the totally mystifying idea that, whereas you are actually doing politics, it is one or several psychoanalytic acts, you will be neck deep in shit and you will be leading people into it. You may believe that what you are saying (or not) is true. But that's your business. In any event, when one does politics, as Lacan and you are doing, it is never without consequences. If you think you are not doing any, wait a little; it will come crashing down on your heads—or rather, and alas, it won't come crashing down on your heads, since you are well protected and know how to lie low. In fact, it will come crashing down on the unfortunates who come to stretch out on your couch and on all their intimates and the intimates of their intimates and on to infinity. In truth, you are all simply cowards, because you are fundamentally, organically irresponsible and never stop talking about responsibility. Keep talking. As for me, I did what I could by coming here, where I have lost a huge amount of time and sacrificed things in– finitely more important than your mumbling. I said it was feeble and infantile, but in fact, you are not even like children; you are like paper pulp on which Lacan writes what he wants. That's it: paper pulp, glue [*colle*] or not, is silent, organically. So long.

Complementary Remarks
on the Meeting of March 15, 1980,
at the Hotel PLM Saint-Jacques[4]

If the accident of my presence at the meeting of Dr. Lacan (Hotel PLM) and his disciples in theory or in analysis led me, for simple and comprehensible reasons (I had been invited on the spot by a friend, who asked me to be present "in order to support us"), to utter a few words, after more than an hour and a half of patience, it was not at all to "assault the Lacan fortress," as she who was not in the auditorium, C. Clément, frivolously writes in a headline in *Le Matin* of March 17. I said nothing against Lacan, against his decision, against his theory, or against the organizations he founded and then dissolved in order to refound them in other new ones, like Freud in former times.

I have always held Lacan (even when he was barely known) for a man of the greatest seriousness who thinks rigorously, something that is not found on every streetcorner these days. That he thinks, moreover, about psychoanalysis—should one say about Freud? or about the idea he has of it? or that he thinks about himself? about whatever pleases him, even if it be baptized the "Freudian field" or the "Freudian cause," Freud being always named as the final reference? On looking at things a bit more closely, however, that reference is not at all sure, that final reference for which Freud's name serves as a pretext, and certain of his concepts (not many), to be sought entirely elsewhere, in names other than that of Freud (for example, Plato, Heidegger, by way of Hegel) and in another "genre or discipline" or "practice," which does not have much to do with psychoanalysis, but a lot to do with what is called "philosophy," and, to boot, "French philosophy," which has been marked in its history since Descartes by the interesting but interested practice of "theoretical tinkering [*bricolage*]."

What then did I do at the meeting called by Lacan that Saturday? If one leaves aside the anecdotal aspects, which, in C. Clément's article in *Le Matin*, are reported rather faithfully although quite partially, and naturally are presented under a sensationalistic and mendacious headline ("Louis Althusser Assaults the Lacan Fortress"), I quite simply performed, "in vivo," an experiment such as I have not frequently done in my life.

And yet, as I said, I have acquired a certain experience from other organizations, that of Action Catholique, in which I was an active militant before the war (and after), then that of the French Communist party, I forgot that of the French and Germany army, in the phony war, then during five years of captivity.[5] While offering certain resemblances (above all with the exercises of collective retreat and meditation, in which each individual takes stock of his states of soul beneath the lowered gaze of a silent god, whose silence no doubt whitens out the garrulous confession of his disciples—I think of those "retreats" done in '38–'39 in a Carthusian monastery at Dombes in the Ain region), this experience of Lacan's signatory disciples literally dumbfounded me.

First, there was no agenda, except that Lacan would speak. It was explained to me that this was appropriate, since Lacan's decision had created some turmoil; it was thus necessary that everyone "get hold of himself" (in the good sense) and, to do so, that contact be reestablished in the presence of Lacan and through it. Granted. I did not hear all of Lacan's speech—I was late—but what I heard did not surprise me, except for a word that troubled me. I thought I heard (but he spoke so softly that one could hardly grasp it) that he was commenting on his deliberately arbitrary decision to dissolve the Ecole in something that was *"like an analytic interpretation."* Others then stepped forward without the precaution of the Lacanian "like" (Lacan, who is prudent, knows how to manipulate or thinks he knows how to manipulate the "like"; example: "the unconscious is structured *like* a language"). There would be a lot to say about that "like," which no doubt governs for Lacan the relation he would like to entertain with his own allusive discourse and his own more or less concealed thought, assuming that he masters them as he thinks he masters them, but which can also throw the first "disciple" of Lacan to come along into the dead end of a confusion of genres and thus of languages, in brief, into Babel (where, as a result of several languages being spoken simultaneously, no one ends up understanding anyone else), with the ensuing concatenation of consequences.

Whatever the case, I had there an unequaled experience. I will skip the details and go to the essential, which can be summarized in three or four remarks.

Why not only the atmosphere of religious meditation (understand me, I have nothing against it) but the endless precautions of the analysts on the podium and on the floor in detailing their moods, their states of soul, regarding Lacan's decision and this blue-gray silent commander? Why were the real issues of the meeting (in any event, what at hearing the analysts remain silent seemed to me the real issues of that meeting so peaceful in its contemplation of the silent master), with a single exception, never indicated or expressed? What issues? I enumerate:

First, issue no. 1, the immediate, juridical, and political one (should one, on the following day, vote in a plenary session for or against dissolving the Ecole?); issue no. 2, which is more important, Lacan's thought (whether it is homogeneous or not; whether it should be criticized, but concerning what, or completed and rectified; etc.); issue no. 3, which is sizable, psychoanalysts' positions in all this (what they believe they are, compared with what they are), their training, and their reasons for going through the Ecole Freudienne, whereas others followed other routes, for there are several roads in the great "Freudian field" for arriving or landing, in full sail or a wreck, on the shore of the father—assuming one be needed, Freud never having been very enthusiastic about the operation; issue no. 4, above all, the crucial issue, it and above all it: the analysands' positions in all this, for it is on them, finally, that everything rests, that is, falls back, and [it is they who] pay, not only in money but in work and birth pangs and mourning, in brief, in the work of analysis, and, as is known, if the analyst doesn't bring all the attention required to his task, things can turn out very badly, or simply stall and lead to an impasse, or end up in a suicide.

C. Clément wrote that I had spoken "in the name of the analysands." That in any event is indeed what I said with great insistence, which was simultaneously a reminder (of the reality of the analysands), an appeal to take into serious consideration the relation at play between analysts and analysands, and also a plea, going from what was almost anger to supplication, if need be, that some account be taken, a proper account, of the worldwide crowd of analysands, millions of men, women, and children, and that they be discussed so that their existence and their problems and the risks they run when they enter into analysis be taken seriously (I am speaking of the risks they run not on their own but as a result of the analyst they go to see, who will use the love transference, once it has "taken," to attempt to allow the analysand to undertake a self-redistribution of the phantasm-affects that were blocking his life).

Now concerning all those issues, the only one dealt with on Saturday was the first, and even then in the form of questions, the analysts who asked those questions ingenuously displaying an ignorance of the elementary principles of French law and of law plain and simple, to the point that one might wonder, since they did not learn these things in school or in books or in the practice of lawyers and suspects, how they were able to miss it "on the couch" of their patients, and whether they are cut off from the world to that extent, or want to be cut off, for reasons that perhaps also pertain to the idea they have of themselves and not only to the division of intellectual labor, as a result of which a jurist can be nothing but a jurist, an analyst an analyst, and so on.

It was thus a question—but against a background of such ignorance!—*only* of the first issue: the juridical one, which will be played out in the effects of the votes of plenary sessions of the Ecole Freudienne, which has not yet been legally dissolved. Concerning the other issues, however, with the exception of a certain disquiet, indeed a disquiet that was certain but that barely surfaced in certain interventions, there was nothing, or at least nothing overt. Which cannot help but raise some strange questions.

Such questions arise above all if one compares this surprising silence with another fact of which I had this disconcerting experience: during the break for cocktails I was able to listen to the same persons, apparently almost all of them practicing analysts, tell me that I was right to intervene, that it had to be done, and that they were in agreement; even more, they had arguments, and they developed them for me. Thus all these loquacious, intelligent, and critical people, who were indeed extremely critical of Lacan so long as it was a matter of saying it to me face-to-face, as if in private, even though it was during the commotion of a recess, those same people (but they hadn't all spoken) had either uttered trifles, stupidities, nonsense, or feeble analyses of their moods regarding the great issues at stake or had shut up, that is, had either shown themselves to be of limited intelligence, indeed confused and even unintelligent, when they took the floor or had simply remained silent, only to speak during the recess.

How might one then think through that astonishing contradiction? Leaving aside the silent ones at the meeting (who, no doubt blasé, knowing in advance whom it was worth dealing with in the meeting, kept their peace for good reason—but that too remains to be seen, for since they remained silent, the reasons for their silence, as well as for their presence there, were kept to themselves), one might wonder whether people intelligent in private, in confidential meetings, and free, and critical do not turn into a religious flock once they are together in public; that's how certain schoolboys behave, gripped by a fear of having to show themselves naked, of speaking before classmates, that is, of showing not what kind of guts they have but whether they have any guts at all—it's what is commonly called shyness. In fact, the reason that they gave me without any difficulty is the same. They told me, "We kept quiet, we keep quiet, because we are afraid." But afraid of whom? For some it was of Lacan; for others, maybe of themselves; and for still others, of I don't know what. And since I asked them, "But if you're afraid (ultimately, of Lacan, of being together, or of yourselves, or of the idea of this or that combination of those reasons), why in hell did you come?" One told me, "It's clear that, if we so want to be afraid, it must reassure us." Well observed.

It is best to stop at this point, since the logic that demands that analyst-intellectuals, who are often very subtle and not racist and "Lacanian" adults, broadly speaking, assemble out of a need to be afraid of Lacan or of X . . . in order to be reassured far transcends analysts, since one can find its equivalent in a number of other organizations—particularly workers' organizations (I mention them because I know them somewhat, but one could just as well invoke the Church or the army), in which the need to be afraid can serve as a reason for belonging to a community of belief, thought, and action, which assures you that you are indeed afraid and are right to be afraid and at the same time reassures you against that fear and its reason, since you are no longer alone as a result of your belonging, which gives you the warmth—be it maternal or any other—of the active and protective group. That this need of fear is today so deep is no doubt a function of the general disorientation of minds in a world (I won't say that it no longer has any meaning: the world never has any) that no longer offers anyone a perspective of the slightest credibility and solidity. So one falls back all the more on the group that satisfies this need for fear and protects against it. An infantile reaction, it will be said? Precisely. Whence the infantile character of the discussion the other day, the feeble and I would even say the almost obscene character of the discussion, for when one indulges one's states of soul by openly and religiously confiding to others the need to understand what one may well mean, when one undresses in public in that way, protected and preserved from all shame, one is asking for only one thing, which is just what one was asking for, namely, to be mothered and to be given a breast from dawn to dusk. In that case, however, things should be called by their name: we are dealing with there something like children regressing to speak a childish language, barely murmured amid the pathos of their half-opened lips, their half-closed eyes, pleading as well, and always murmured-sung like a complaint, or rather (since they are damned adults [*sacrés adultes*] and even consecrated one [*adultes sacrés*]), they are adults who infantilize themselves in order to beg, in an infinite and hopeless prayer, for the "Mother" they need to satisfy their need to be afraid. That "Mother" possibly could be Lacan, as well as the colleagues present in the session on Saturday, those who are in a position to listen and, given the reigning silence, to hear. That "Mother" can also be the one who speaks and who then treats himself as a child but also as a "Mother" through his public plaint-complaint, thus moving as a "Mother" to confront the questions he addresses to himself as a child. Ultimately this public "child-Mother" dialogue can be mute. On Saturday we saw a few people take the floor to say, "I am speaking, but it is because I have nothing to say (other than my moving desire to say it and to be heard)," and even a person get up to speak and say nothing at all. I am purposely saying "Mother" because Lacan thinks far too much from the perspective of the "Father," and—but I don't want to advance on this mined terrain—his students or disciples of the other day think a bit too much of Lacan as a "Father-Master" of everything, words, truth, knowledge, and so on, whereas in the discreet psychodrama at the PLM, the express demand of almost all was a demand for the "Mother," at least the demand of almost all those who spoke.

If one thinks that one can extricate oneself by invoking the unconscious phantasms of this or that individual, or of thinking in categories pertaining only to the practice of therapy, that is, to the negotiation of the analytic transference by the analyst and the analysand, I say that such a claim is obscurantism pure and simple. It is too clear that phantasms were at work that Saturday, at that meeting with no object other than the staging of the need (yes, I write *need* and not only desire, wish, or unconscious phantasm; yes, I write need and I specify preconscious—or even conscious—need) to be afraid before the "Mother," but it is also all too clear that it was not just any phantasms but those that were "summoned" (all the disciples by the master) by the situation of a "public complaint" or assault on decency required in order to allow oneself to be consoled and reassured and, ultimately, mothered and protected by the "mother," or rather her phantasm, whose bearers or "objects" of cathexis Lacan and, consequently, the others present (or absent) are par excellence. One needed that material gathering, that assembling of very particular *"parlêtres"* [speech beings] (!) who are the "Lacanian" analysts in a meeting in a deluxe hotel, but without an agenda, and in the expectation of who knows what coming from Lacan or, should nothing come (and nothing came), in the expectation of who knows what coming from being together, quite simply human warmth, indeed the odor of male and female. In truth, behind that material and maternal, mothering, self-mothering convocation, exuding mother (and not at all woman) through all its pores, there were extremely serious things: *for example*, the gradual crisis, for long years, but finally exploded, of the Ecole Freudienne; *for example*, the need of Lacan, who could no longer bear them, to exclude those "admitted forgers" about whom he spoke in writing—and whom J.-A. Miller, who is said to be the successor designate of the master to think and help think when he will no longer be, named by their names (well known to some)—(since the statutes did not foresee any sanction, and thus exclusion, the breakup of the Ecole becomes, in Lacan's hands, the disguised form, under cover of a theoretical reassertion of authority, of exclusion); *for example*, the conflict publicly engaged among analysts on the world scale (J.-A. Miller was right when he said on Saturday that what is happening is a small historical event, to be sure, but it is happening on a planetary scale) concerning Lacan's thought (whether it holds up; whether it's a theory, a thought, a philosophy, or philosophy; what it bears on; how it deals with what it bears on; whether one should be for or against it, and if the former, completely for or with critical reservations—then again, the question might be poorly posed; etc.); *for example*, the question of analysts in general, their relation to Freud and to Lacan, or others (M. Klein, Winnicott, etc.), the (very thorny) question (which poisons all "societies") of the training of analysts, the question of the differences in therapeutic technique, and so on, so many questions on which everyone knows that among analysts, on the world scale, there are divisions and conflicts going to the point of open scission, the decision of a single individual (Lacan) to dissolve his Ecole, and so on; and *for example* (and finally), the question of the analysands, of which there are perhaps millions in the world, and the price they have to pay (I'm not even speaking of the money they have to fork out) as much to accomplish their own work as analysands (the often atrocious and always very difficult and testing "*Durcharbeiten*," at the edge of abysses, often on the brink of suicide) as to "absorb" (since it happens frequently) the analyst's responses and nonresponses, including the unconscious effects of countertransference, indeed the analyst's acting out—in brief, all the signs that, wanting to or not, the analyst gives them for free, the analyst at whose mercy they are, without any witness or recourse in the world and quite often unprotected, that is, unprotected in relation not to themselves but to the analyst, of whom they know that he too is a man, and particularly, given the stakes, vulnerable to doing or saying nonsense, not so much because "he allows himself to be authorized only by himself " (everyone does as much ultimately, whether he be free or a slave, provided that the conditions be there) as because he does not truly allow himself to be authorized by himself but does so only by the thinking of this one or that, for example, of Lacan. Thus, assuming that the analyst in question has truly heard that self-authorization through Lacan's thought, which presupposes that this thought is comprehensible, in its literality and in its theoretico-formalist pretension—it is no more than the internalization of a thought, that of Lacan, to which the analyst refers himself and within which he believes he can find the truth within his reach, both about Freud and the therapies he is conducting. The truth! Yes, Lacan's thought offers itself as the truth both about psychoanalysis and of psychoanalysis, that is, as a truth more true than the one found in Freud's texts, a proper revision that succeeds this time and that goes further than Freud, a truth of Freud's thought (assuming that the term *thought* is appropriate to Freud's writings) that goes further than Freud in theory and further as well in its "technique" of using the transference, whence the sessions without preestablished length, without a contract determining length, as if the analyst were alone able to impose his own measure of length (and why wouldn't it be the analysand, if that is how one is reasoning, who would impose his own?). As if the analyst were not caught, his hands tied up, paralyzed in the countertransference, as if he were able to be the sole judge of things, deciding that today three minutes are enough—but for whom? For him, to be sure, since he decides by himself (and even then, it is not so sure), and sometimes but not always for the other as well (but this case will always seem suspect to any experienced analyst). Who will decide in the debate in which the "Lacanian" analyst, following the master, is alone in disposing of the language and the use of discretionary decision making, being, as one likes to say but above all to joke in the (Communist) party, "unitary for two"? Of course, in the Lacanian system it is the analyst alone, trusting his "insight"; it happens by flair, the flair of a single individual. Will you say that it could have been negotiated? With difficulty, since one would be given over to the patient's "demand"; moreover, the negotiation takes place in "classical" pre-Lacanian practice. It takes place in the form of the contract proposed by the analyst and explicitly accepted by the patient . . .

5

Correspondence with Jacques Lacan

1963–1969

THIS EXCHANGE OF LETTERS *begins at a crucial moment in the life of Jacques Lacan: he had just been stricken from the list of training analysts of the Société Française de Psychanalyse (SFP) on October 13, 1963, after two years of negotiations with representatives of the International Psychoanalytical Association (IPA). Stripped of the right to train students, Lacan was then obliged to break with the official institution,*[1] *which plunged him into great turmoil, evidence of which can be seen in his first letters.*

For his part, Louis Althusser published that same year in the Revue de l'enseignement philosophique *(13, no. 5 [July 1963]) an article, "Philosophie et sciences humaines," in which he praised Lacan. The two men had not yet met—and that would not occur, in fact, until the beginning of December 1963, as these letters and Althusser's diary, conserved in his archives, indicate; quite plausibly they met in the course of a dinner on December 3.*

Finally, to situate this epistolary exchange, it should be noted that Lacan delivered his last lecture at Sainte-Anne on "les noms du père" [the names of the father] on the very day on which he would write, at night, his first letter to Louis Althusser and that it was through Althusser's intervention that he would make his entry at the Ecole Normale Supérieure on January 15, 1964, with a first lecture on "excommunication."[2]

These letters of Lacan and Althusser were discovered in the archives of Louis Althusser. Those of Lacan, eight in number, are all handwritten and composed on stationery measuring 13.5 cm by 20.5 cm, with a heading on the right mentioning the address of 5 rue de Lille and a telephone number, with the exception of a postcard (no. 8) sent from Greece and the last letter (no. 12) written on a blank sheet of standard size. Since it was impossible to have access to the originals of Althusser's letters and thus to possible handwritten marginal additions, the text of his letters has been established following typed duplicates that Althusser kept in a folder marked "Lacan," along with the latter's letters.

It has seemed useful to us to add to this exchange the text of a long letter (no. 5) that Althusser had also typed but finally chose not to send—as he himself confirms in the letter to Franca of January 21, 1964, cited in the introduction to this volume. It will be noted in this regard that the Althusser archives contain numerous unsent letters to numerous correspondents and that they turn out in almost every case to be extremely interesting. The one we are publishing in this volume will thus arrive at its destination, but posthumously . . .

O. C.

Correspondence with Jacques Lacan

1. Jacques Lacan to Louis Althusser

This Wednesday, no, Thursday 21-XI-63

Our relations are old, Althusser. You surely remember that lecture I gave at Normale after the war,[1] a crude rudiment for a dark time (one of the actors in my present drama found his path there, nevertheless); for the rest, your somewhat impressionistic judgment was "reported" to me some time after.

The one that now comes to me from the (June–July) *Bulletin de l'enseignement philosophique*,[2] I would be ungracious to decline the honor, and I thank you for allowing this testimony to be heard at a juncture in which, to be sure, I have no reason to doubt my enterprise, but in which, all the same, a stupid wind is raging over my very fragile skiff.

I have put an end to this seminar in which I tried for ten years to trace the paths of a dialectic whose invention was for me a marvelous task.

I had to. It grieves me.

And then I think of all those gravitating in your vicinity and of whom I am told that they held in esteem what I did—which was not for them, nonetheless.

I am thinking this evening or, rather, early this morning, of those friendly faces . . . Something should be said to them. I would like you to come visit me, Althusser.

J. Lacan

2. Louis Althusser to Jacques Lacan

[Paris] 26.XI.63

Dear Lacan,

Thank you from the bottom of my heart. Your word, your thought, and your sympathy touch me deeply.

You are not alone. I am speaking not only of the analysts who owe you everything: their number is great, and they are often the best. I am speaking also of those who, in contesting you, nevertheless follow you willingly or not, constrained by the truth you have brought to light. I am speaking also of those who, from the outside, have discovered and recognized you.

I have already spoken (and have had others speak) about you in this house for six years.[3] I know you came here a very long time ago. I was at the time a prisoner returning from Germany, a convalescent kept far from the Ecole, and concerning your lecture all I heard was the stir it made and the repercussions it had. This year the discourse I am conducting about you is at the heart of a collective labor to whose rigor I subject (with their agreement) all those whom the subject affects. We have had a very good beginning.[4]

I regard you as being, in the field one is provisionally obliged to call the "human sciences," the first thinker who has assumed the theoretical responsibility of giving to Freud veritable concepts worthy of him—and to that extent the first to have accorded that "domain" the path of access, the only one, that might be expected of Freud: a *forbidden* path. That interdiction, insofar as it is forbidden, is the path of access itself. I have been thinking this for several years. I am now in a position, at least I believe so, to give proof of it with reasons precise and rigorous enough for me to run the risk of publishing them.

I have been pursuing obscure works on Marx for some fifteen years. I have finally, slowly, laboriously, emerged from the night. Things are clear to me now. That austere inquiry, that long and harsh gestation, was needed.

When I managed to see clearly in Marx, at the time I found myself able to give Marx's *wild* dialectic (wild not because he didn't "have the time," as fools say, to tame it and to enclose it in his theory but because, like Freud later on, he was subject to the condition of having to produce his thought within the matter of a work that was nonphilosophical in its object, because that philosophical thought "in its practical state" in that work was precisely reduced to a "wild" state by the historical constraint of concepts imposed by his time, Hegelian ones, the only ones then available and handy)—at the time, then, when I found myself able to give to Marx's thought (I am speaking emphatically of his "philosophy," and not of his work: *Capital*) its *theoretical form*, it was then that I saw myself on the threshold of understanding you.

Previously I had certainly felt and then grasped the interest of your theoretical investigations, but I had grasped it only in its relation to Freud. I can say now that it has bearing (in a paradoxical form: that of interdiction, or *absolute discontinuity*) well beyond Freud. I will reveal it one day soon, hoping not to betray you, when I will show, precisely, that *beyond*. I will then explain in what and why your attempt implies (in the paradoxical form of absolute discontinuity) the theoretical absolute of the enabling conditions of Marx. That is what I wanted to communicate, in advance, in abbreviated form, by speaking of Marx's revolution (rejection of *homo economicus*, rejection of any philosophical "subject") and of Freud's revolution, which you have restored, if not given, to us (rejection of any *homo psychologicus)*. When I was able to utter that simple word, everything was clear. I believe I understand that this line has fulfilled its purpose if it is true that it has allowed you to judge whether I had, on an *essential* point, encountered your intention.

To be sure, I work in a domain apparently quite removed from your own. Let us abandon those appearances. I am doing my best in my "domain" to combat the very adversaries who would like to reduce you to silence, to *their* silence. I speak of your theoretical work and of the *beyond* on which it touches. You will have allies, have no fear, and I can see a large number of them already among the people who still don't know you, whom you no doubt didn't think you were addressing so directly; all those will shove down the throat of the pseudo-"psychologists" and other philosophers of the "human person" and "intersubjectivity," as well as the technocrats of "structuralism," their pretensions, their sermons, and their amateurism: in sum, their theoretical imposture. We shall together take some joy in this, the joy of reason finally "at home" in its most disconcerting and intimate objects. I am prophesying, but we have entered, in large measure thanks to you, into an era in which one can finally be a prophet in one's own country. I have no merit in running the risk of this prophecy; henceforth we have a right to it, since we possess the means for it, in this country at last become *ours*.

You can imagine what pleasure I will have in meeting you. But I am presently in the (temporary) situation of having to bear a large part of the weight of the Ecole. We have a marvelous director,[5] but he has been here for only two months; we no longer have an assistant director.[6] I help the former in part of his work, and I take over the functions of the latter, and then my own in addition—I mean work of general administration. In addition, I am in charge (I am more attached to this than anything else) of studies in philosophy (philosophers are proliferating at an astonishing pace in the house), and I must, of course, maintain my role in teaching and research.

Let us allow some time to pass, time enough for this situation to be transformed. We will see each other then, and I will be able to tell you of the state of the work and research of which you are the center.

I am sending you under the same cover a text written last spring. It speaks of concepts and characters entirely foreign, to all appearances, to your problems. You will see, however, where I was, as though in a mirror, and you will be able perhaps to infer where I am presently, assuming that I have advanced a bit in the meanwhile. I don't need to tell you that the text appeared in *La Pensée*[7] and that I had to start with the rudiments.

I extend to you my best wishes for your work. You will know that our expectations of you are still infinite.

I communicate to you the very high esteem in which I hold you.

[Louis Althusser]

3. Jacques Lacan to Louis Althusser

This Saturday, December 1, 1963

Very dear friend,

What precious testimony your letter constitutes for me.

That at the distance at which you are what I address to one close by, often opaque, manages to make itself understood is justification for the faith I *seem* to accord (to the point of disconcerting some) to the pure act of saying—to the sole fact of having said (they are the ones who express themselves like that).

Your article[8]—I am reading it. It fascinates me, and I discover my questions in it.

But the urgency remains that makes it imperative for me to ask you for the hour I requested of you the other day.

So, at your convenience. I will call Monday.

Your

J. L.

4. Louis Althusser to Jacques Lacan

Dear Lacan,   *Paris, December 4, '63*

I thought a good deal about our conversation since yesterday.[9] I had many other things to tell you, but we will no doubt have the time and the opportunity. A bit of leisure is needed to broach them. But you are caught up, and it's quite understandable, not in the urgency of the impossible situation that has been inflicted on you but in its subjective as well as objective effects. An outside witness, above all from outside the world that has been the object of your efforts, can only give you his sympathy and his understanding. I fear that those sentiments will hardly help you and that you will be alone in the face of your bitterness.

All that I can offer you: a few reflections spoken out loud, precisely in the name of the *exteriority* that constitutes the witness that I am.

My question: what did they understand of your discourse—a question that others (and first of all Delay) must have had to repeat. That question has a very profound meaning for me. I will tell you why: it calls into question the issue of the access to theory (that of any discipline whatever: I am treating a very general question) of those who are plunged into the horizon of a practice, either because they pursue it or because they are, dare I say, its material. A very, very particular practice, because before you that theory did not exist. How can one accede, from the very heart of a practice pursued or experienced, blindly pursued or experienced, to its *concept*? A problem of pedagogy, it will be said, but in the last analysis it is not a problem of pedagogy. It's an entirely different problem that concerns the transition from what I would call a "practical truth" (which is practiced or experienced) to the theory of that truth or to its concept. Now this problem is, at bottom, a specific—and crucial—theoretical problem. You have admirably shown that problems of analytic technique cannot be resolved at the level of technique, that a *leap* was needed—the recourse to theory—and that in the final analysis only theory decides and determines problems of technique; what does that mean? Does it mean that there is, on the one hand, pure and simple technique, which would be only technique, practiced by people without any idea of theory and to whom that theory must be taught so that they can then reform their technique? That is not the way things go. The conflict is not between a pure technique *without theory* and pure theory. There is no pure technique, and that too you have shown. Any technique that wants to be pure technique is, in fact, an *ideology* of technique, that is, a false theory. Moreover, that is indeed what your effort implies: you are not one who teaches people who are only technicians that they are simply *blind*, or ignorant, quite simply by teaching them of the existence and the necessity of a theory; you are one who teaches allegedly pure "technicians" the truth of their practice on the absolute condition of destroying something other than an ignorance or blindness—by which I mean an ideology, the false theory that is the obligatory mate of their false innocence as pure technicians. Every pedagogy thus cannot consist in teaching a truth to one who is ignorant, thus filling a void with a plenum—every pedagogy consists of substituting an explicit and true theory for an implicit and false theory, *replacing* a spontaneous ideology (in the Leninist sense, in the sense in which man, whether a union member or an analyst, is by nature an *ideological animal*—that expression is not Lenin's) with a scientific theory. Now what distinguishes an explicit and conscious scientific theory from the implicit and spontaneous ideology it must *replace* is a radical *discontinuity*. In a precise sense, it can be said that pedagogy has nothing of a phenomenology, even a *disguised* one: there is no internal *transition* from ideology to science. Every pedagogy is necessarily a *break*, and to be something other than a compromise or an illusion, it must be pursued within the conscious forms of that *break*. (I take the term *phenomenology*, you will understand me, in its Hegelian sense, in the sense of the immanent development of consciousness, from its elementary-originary forms, which negate themselves as elementary-originary in and from the outset of their first position-pretension, until its higher forms, which for Hegel are already "in germ" in the first.) Traditional pedagogy registers that theoretical imperative in its forms of *practical* existence, if only in the institutional distance separating teachers from students, etc. I won't insist. Those forms may be aberrant in their metamorphoses; they are, as the very existence of the break in essence between ideology and knowledge, essential to the truth of the essence of all pedagogy. That those forms remained at a practical level, without being the object of *reflection*, is the defining characteristic of the pedagogy of most, if not all, dissemination of knowledge at present. That the *nonreflection* of those forms of break, which grounds every pedagogy of a science in the inevitable element of ideology, that the *nonconcept* of those forms of rupture or break—in other words, the lack of an explicit and theoretical thematization of those essential forms of break—can, *in certain cases*, seriously harm the science that is precisely the object of the pedagogy in question is clarity itself. In certain precise cases the theory of pedagogy, and thus the theory of the break (or of the absolute discontinuity existing between science and ideology), must be theoretically developed and spelled out, since it is organically part of the *science* that is, precisely, to be taught. I know from experience of a case in which that theorization of the pedagogy of a science as an integral, indispensable part of the very science it is a question of teaching is absolutely indispensable to the theoretical practice of that science: it is *philosophy* (note that this thematization is, in my opinion, indispensable to every theoretical pedagogy—but that imperative is not acknowledged, except in philosophy, or at least by certain philosophers). The history of philosophy shows that the problem has long (and since Plato himself) been consciously raised by the great philosophers—raised, if not resolved, since all their solutions are mythical, but at least they raised the problem. The mythical solution par excellence, which denies what allows the very positing of the problem—in other words, the *theory* of the positing of the problem in the very form that excludes not only its solution but its own positing—is Hegel's phenomenology. I skip ahead here; this point—which is, moreover, exciting—is too easy to develop.

You know the *other* example: psychoanalysis. Everything you have told me about your current research concerning the desire of the analyst goes in this direction. It is the *encounter*, in specific forms and structures, with this problem, by the psychoanalyst, in his own self-image, but generally not as an object of reflection. You are in the process of reflecting on that encounter (and many other things!) in your current research. I consequently suspect that you will understand what I am getting at.

I was extremely struck by your response: "What I say to them says something to them, codifies, transforms their attitude, their recognition of reality, their way of approaching analytic reality." You were saying it at once about the analysts who listened to you and the analysands (in analysis) who listened to you. They threw back at you that, in sum, this was an analyst's intervention about his patients, that the public and apparently impersonal—and thus objective—forms of the intervention (which was entirely theoretical, all theory) might serve as an alibi or a mask, etc., for an intervention experienced as real by members of your audience then in analysis. I am collecting phenomena even from the odious arguments with which you are countered, without those phenomena ever being able, in my eyes, to serve as an argument against you. From all this I retain the following (which at first sight seems to be rather disparate): that it is you who uttered the words, the master words of the situation. Those who listened to you, from the very depth of their "experience"—whether analysts, practitioners, or analysands, the "practitioned," each in his place as subject-object of practice, of a common experienced but *unthought* practice, since the *thoughts* of the analyst practitioners were in fact as little *thoughts* as those of the analyzed—all those auditors of the *concept* you were giving them, of the concept of the practice they lived, all those auditors had no right to the *concept* of break implied in your enterprise.

If I am saying something scandalous here, you will correct me. I shall explain. Their *general* theoretical ignorance, that is, their ignorance of the existence and the imperative *of theory überhaupt* (without any consideration of content) was such, that is, their lack of *theoretical* training in general was such (and the culprit must be, if not current university teaching, then the empiricist pedagogy of medicine, etc.), that the enterprise of having them make a transition from their "living experience" to its own theory was a quasi-hopeless enterprise, *pedagogically speaking* (according to the essence of all pedagogy), that the undertaking of taking them by the hand from their own experience and their own practical situation, of showing them the outline of the very theory of that practice, was an objectively quasi-hopeless undertaking. One does not pass without a break from a practice to its concept, from experience to its concept. This illusion has been thematized by well-known philosophies, such as Hegel's formerly and more recently Husserl's and Merleau's. I say thematized, that is, accepted and expressed in concepts, in the very concepts produced by that illusion, thus in illusory concepts. That, fundamentally, was Merleau's path. That is why it never crossed your own, in theory, I mean. That is why Merleau, who needed (and no doubt for vital reasons, which appear well in Sartre's admirable article on him in *Les Temps modernes*, where you were alone [*seul*][10] in treating that great deceased figure in a manner worthy of him, that is, by speaking of him as though he were still *alive*)[11] that security of continuity, never succeeded in achieving that beginning of understanding what is at stake in psychoanalysis; his theory of it is aberrant and aberrantly disarming in its theoretical infantilism (I take the term in its almost technical sense: there was at the bottom of it all a certain unresolved relation with his mother). Merleau thought that from "experience" to its concept there was a path traced, *emerging from experience itself*, like Ruth's tree from the entrails of Boaz or like the child from his mother's womb (the image of Boaz: it's something else—the placenta, the cord, it's something else). This myth of a path that in the very night is inscribed by essence to lead to the daylight, which is already the outline and the imminence of the day, its promise, its ripening future, this myth of deaf and tender spring keeping vigil and growing in the dead of winter until May comes, this myth of the sun keeping watch in the night itself, simply hidden by the other side of the earth, its other opaque with its very presence, and appearing at dawn as what it was in the shadows, those shadows that are only light (Feuerbach, who had taken the idea I don't know where—do you?—said that opaque bodies are only light, but in the form of infinitesimal light, that finally, essence never has an opposite, since its opposite is only itself in alienated form)—so here I am no doubt far from Merleau but very close to the illusion of those who, not reflecting on the break they should be able to know, or of those who don't reflect on it because they are not yet at the point of suspecting it, that spontaneous myth in which men commonly represent their relation to their knowledge in the form of their nonrelation to its real conditions, that myth that represents to them their wish for a future without history, without break, without the imaginary of a past that has led them to where they are and that *is not cut off from them,* that imaginary myth in which men, every day, embody their umbilical theoretical security

(philosophers and their mothers, a good subject for a thesis, the idealist philosophers, I mean), that myth defines the real condition of most
of those who teach a body of knowledge to those who listen to them.

That both groups might be analysts to boot no doubt adds something essential to the mix.

I return to your audience. That condition: everything in your teaching, and, what is more, in its very *form*, is its denunciation. To be sure,
you brought to those who came to receive them from you the results
of a fishing expedition in which each could recognize, from a distance
at first, then closer up, his own favorite rockfish and all the dark cap-
tives of the deep. They were still alive in the net of words. They were
yours, but also theirs: multiple fish, and all communed in the public evidence of that proliferation. Yes, they saw that it was their own reserves
that you were bringing back to the surface, in those mute and sprightly
beings, without perceiving that one can catch anything in a net except
the sea. Concerning the sea, you wanted to tell them in a desperate effort that it was there, in its products, and more than the sea, the sky that
dominated them, that oppressive layer of air without weight, so light to
human respiration that men move in it as in the very liquid of their
stare, their voice, without problem, that is, without ever making contact with its problem: that absence of contact, more than the sea or the
earth beneath them, supporting their paces and their bodies, and their
very contentment, thus, to their very heart. You warned them with numerous great cries, denouncing the illusion of their peace, all the illusions bearing the names of our enemies: bitter cries suspecting that
they were often for your audience no more than a mania that one had
to allow you, the cost of your freedom, not necessarily the condition
of their freedom. Your very language, those turns that they reproached
you for, that way of saying in which some who wish you well see the
reminder of primordial articulation, in the strangeness of a snapshot in
which they suddenly see themselves stared at by a truth that does not
return their gaze, in which their very gaze encounters in your words
its own void (the stare of their dead eye, which they thought alive),
their garrulous ear, its own radical deafness—your very language was a
warning, a desperate warning. Those who wish you well hear in that
disconcerting silence what they understand as the language of the
Other, thus rendered almost present, offstage, among them. They don't
see me, but I am among them. They don't hear me, and yet I speak to
them. There too their own experience sought and found itself in an

ordeal in which it was a question of something entirely else: a theoretical *break*, and not an allegory of silence.

In brief, that is how I see your public. It is not from within but *from without* that one can announce that a *break* has come, that the break is consummated, and that one must, to understand the very interiority one is living, *begin by it*. This idea, or rather this concept of an absolute (theoretical) exteriority as the enabling condition of a theoretical understanding of interiority itself, is something they had at bottom no desire to receive from you. They have remained in their inside. They think they've got enough for ten years; they never go too far in search of the pleasure of returning home, or rather, when one has traveled a bit, one is happy to take a stroll in the forest at Compiègne, since after all, barely has one left the city and there are the same trees, and the country, and the air, the air! the same air everywhere. They never go too close by in search of the pleasure of returning home. They never go too close by in search of the pleasure (the security) of *staying at home*.

Could you do more? They would undoubtedly have chased you sooner. And those very warnings through which, talking to them about Hegel and Plato, and philosophy, you hoped to indicate to them that there is a place for theory, that it has its topos, that it has its home, which was not theirs, those very warnings were perhaps also taken for one of your manias, which you had to be forgiven, since it was you, while waiting for it to pass; those references also flattered their need for security, their need not to be alone but to have witnesses on the outside, great witnesses to reassure that anxious ground of their soul which asks only for security and not knowledge. That Ricoeur so moved them[12] I see as a sign that they were above all looking not for the knowledge you wanted to impose on them but for simple recognition, which can, to be sure, take the moving form (but what relation?) of an honest man telling of his relations with psychoanalysis, that is, with his own ignorance. Merleau, Ricoeur, perhaps others soon, gratifications, with the advantage of a certified university label, what the hell, philosophy, which has its officials just as psychiatry has its Delays—with generosity into the bargain, and sincerity, even when one is at the Collège [de France], or one allows oneself to be carried there one day. You were speaking to them about the existence of theory while speaking to them about Hegel and Plato. They understood that for all eternity they were not alone and that, as a result, they could together enjoy the security of the testimony of their existence. You know: that old proof of the existence of God through universal consent, which one sees in certain humanists of the fifteenth century take the form—worthy of their intellectual aristocracy—of proof by *the consent of Great Authors.*

Could you do more? You were, whatever you did, for them, *someone from the inside.* At the limit bearing witness about an outside, about the outside. Agreed. But they had in advance delegated to you the portfolio of External Relations without themselves going to take a look. You were their guarantor. They acknowledged that portfolio and that function in you, but on the tacit (radical) condition that you leave them the hell alone by leaving them at home. They let you arrange things, that is, the inside, their inside, their interiority, their "interior," yes, and then, when they felt that the situation was adequate like that, that you were becoming an annoyance, that they had heard enough, that it looked good, a look that *classified* them, they proceeded in such manner that one day the door would be slammed in your face. That is in order. Not the order of reasons, that is, of Reason, but of proprieties. One has to think of the future, that is, of the present.

All this to give some meaning to what, at the end of our conversation, when we were walking through the streets before the tobacco stands closed, I was saying to you precisely *about the outside.* Yes, there is an outside, thank God. And one day, willingly or unwillingly (unwillingly, but they will manage one day to put a good face on it), they will have to recognize directly, without an intermediary charged with that impossible mission, without being able to depend on someone who was protecting them from the outside that he was announcing, that such an outside exists.

Outside. You are henceforth outside. In your true place: that of your reasons, of Reason.

There, you are not alone.

It is enough to begin working—you who have not stopped working—it is enough to begin working with those who are working within that outside.

A simple question of organization of work. It can be arranged. There are precedents.

Yours,

[Louis Althusser]

5. Louis Althusser to Jacques Lacan[13]

Paris, Tuesday, December 10 [1963], 6 P.M.

Dear Lacan,

Your silence has a great value for me. I expected it.

You could have answered me, or rather someone very different from you could have answered me, while avoiding the question of the text.[14] You, no. You have all the art and talent needed to settle a question with a word, to chase off flies, bores, or gossips. But you are not a man to throw words as fodder at things, even if only to get rid of them. You know that a word or a silence, when it is the pertinent word or silence, literally the last word—which can be silence—is the same thing. Yes, the last word on a thing is the thing itself. And when the thing is at its last word, that is, at the point at which the only word that one can confer on it is one that confirms its extremity, that of its bare evidence, of its very existence, then one rediscovers the origin at the point of its birth: its own abyss at the moment it denies it in order to be.

Your silence is priceless.

You will understand that I am addressing the author of your writings, the thought that inhabits them and that can indeed laugh at the affectations and the baseness that historical stupidity, the ideological stupidity of the time, sly exercises in vengeance, rancor, the desperate revenge of little men that it has *marked* (yes, as you say so well, that desire is *marked*)—that the historically inevitable ideological stupidity of the present conjuncture has organized against you. Your thought will live, will grow, and these dwarfs will return to their proper measure: boxwood hedges cut back that have for eternity been ordered to protect the flowerbeds of the walkways of Saint-Anne from no one at all. Everyone ignores them, no one sees them, not even the gardener who shaves their head four times a year. And yet individuals who walk and occasionally have thoughts pass down those paths every day. Protect me from images of indignation, since they are not appropriate; they lower the debate, which I refuse to reduce to the ludicrous conditions of those who opened it.

I shall speak another language to you, that of your work. For it is you, to be sure, a man too well known for me to know him—and whom, moreover, I do not know (as one says "to know" when speaking of an "acquaintance": he is or isn't an "acquaintance" of "mine")—

who was speaking to me the other evening. I heard you, and I believe I have given you (without my ever having to "lend" you my attention, as one says, since it was returned in advance, and you don't suspect how much) signs; I heard you, as one sometimes hears harmonics of strings repeat on another stave the melody one is playing. I heard you in two keys.

In the key of your present personal tragedy, a tragedy since the children of your voice have cut your throat, and you know that they're its children and have committed this crime; since you have refused, alone, bloodied, to accept the only act they abandoned to you: to abandon to you that abandonment called despair, which is death in life itself, a public death without an identifiable murder, which would have given them all the profit of the crime without the risks of sanction (there are others aside from the legal kind). You remained alone, and I, who do not "know" you, I could be nothing other than the witness of that solitude, of your courage and of your pride.

Had I heard you only in that key, I would merely have been one more in a long list of impotent witnesses to historical tragedies, which, at times, bear names other than those of Madrid and Barcelona. Those witnesses occasionally recount their memories later on, a helpless film or narrative, as tragic as what they saw, with the distance that renders their intolerable testimony tolerable to nonwitnesses—to nonwitnesses and to the witnesses themselves. It is no doubt not by chance—Nietzsche had sensed it in a miraculous moment before falling into the abyss of cries of suffering—that witnesses of the tragic can bear their memory, that is, their suffering, only on the condition of making of it a *work to see*. What they saw they want others to see as well, in images, so that they might no longer be alone, so that the solitude that is the tragic itself might finally end for them in its public sharing, so that a *public* spectacle (since a book is something read *alone*) might be imposed on men, beneath the fiction and the lure of art, might, then, be shared, and destroyed in that sharing, the unspeakable and intolerable solitude that has marked them forever. Outside that sharing there is no recourse for them other than the public venting of their suffering, so that, at the least (one never knows), others might hear them; they will no longer be alone in howling their loneliness, like those wounded dogs that wander over the long plains at night and that howl only at night, since by day they would be able to *see* that no one hears them. The howl of that suffering is a book: Nietzsche himself, who was haunted by the crowds communing publicly in the works of Wagner but who knew, with a prodigious awareness, that is, an unconsciousness, that certain howls need the protection of the night (a book: not *seeing* who reads it, one doesn't see, one will not see, and until the end one will live in that desperate hope that it isn't read; one will live out of the belief that it is perhaps read, truly read, *understood by one or two who have acquired it*). The author of *The Birth of Tragedy*, the man who had understood in a flash that he was forever the witness of the tragic and forever marked by its seal, that of solitude, also knew that he was forever forbidden from delivering himself of the frightening spectacle of the tragic whose witness he had been, in a *spectacle*, since he had been its witness not in the flesh but in reason, having experienced the tragedy of understanding what the tragic was; what remained to him was only the night of a book, of books, in which to howl to all men that solitude, which is suffering itself, the abyss of living in the night, in order to keep the hope that another *would hear him*. The voice, when it says the tragic and says it in the night, is but a howl, a long howl that no longer stops in order to give until the end, until the final instant, a chance to its hope, that is, to its despair, of ever being heard.

Thank God I am writing to you; so you have remained silent. I also heard you in a different key—you were thus also speaking in a different key. Your silence: it was that in you a discourse other than the howl of indignation and bitterness continued, alive, giving to the man you are the reason and the courage of that silence. (Oedipus kept his silence; that is, he spoke, and he spoke about the flowers and brooks he no longer saw, he spoke of something else; in him there spoke a reason, a true one, perhaps the first in the world, the one that Nietzsche, deafened by his own suffering, did not hear, that he, for his part, forever confused with the reasoning cowardice of Socrates, not having been able to hear—you know why—that reason to which his prehistory as a man had made him deaf, that reason through which, in the very spectacle of tragedy, a man named Sophocles indicated to all men, and to us, for the first time in the world, that art can be something other than a refuge, and the spectacle of tragedy can be something entirely other than a sharing of suffering: the very birth of reason.)

Yes, I heard in you another discourse. It is not by chance, I repeat, that you spoke to me about your work on the analyst's desire. I would have doubted—God forbid! but after all, a tragedy can truly overwhelm, for a time at least, the most courageous of men—that you would have given me, in a dazzling flash, proof that not only was nothing in you breached but that you were already at the very point at which the battle (which some think or perhaps regret they have won so quickly) is joined, the point at which no one, except for you, and perhaps me, is aware that the battle will be played out. You had two words that were also two flashes (and when those flashes traverse the night, there is no more night—in truth, there is no night for you; you have no need of it as the accomplice of a despair you have rejected from the beginning). A work on the marriage of the analyst, of a specific analyst, and his affairs and political obsessions. That was enough. Then a word on the desire of the analyst. That time, no doubt, was any longer possible.

You've got the adversary by the throat; you've got the very ones who wanted to deprive you of a voice, and naturally, they don't suspect it. That is in order. Their weakness will have to betray them. Weakness is always paid for, when one knows how to strike it at its weak point, in that ultimate point where it is nothing but weakness. Armor (which can also be covered with heraldry and emblems, armor, which is not only armorial bearings): on the last day, it covers only bare flesh, belly and throat. Ever since they have been fighting, men have known this, and they have related their great fear in tales of combat in which the great themselves no longer have anything left with which to counter the entrails of death except the last rampart of all the protections in the world: a bit of metal to which an artisan, in the noisy sunlight of a forge, gave the awkward form of a man, that ludicrous death of steel in order to preserve the despair of a body, which was alive because naked. That weak point, their weakness itself, the public armor of those undressed pseudo-kings whom you have discovered. They are already defeated and are dying. You have continued on your path, toward other battles, life, in sum.

Here is how I would make the reason that speaks in you speak: rather, I let it speak, being only its voice, doing no more than scan, as you have said on other occasions, the discourse that it has already uttered, and for a long time, since it is never anything but a single discourse that you have been conducting for twenty years.

The analyst's desire. You sought it in *The Symposium*.[15] In fact, you were searching in *The Symposium* for the illusion of the analyst's desire about itself, Plato having given voice, in the form of a formally irreproachable discourse (if one insists on it, and one can legitimately insist on it), solely to those illusions he wanted to make men recognize as the opposite of illusion. I don't know what you derived from *The Symposium*; I would have to reread it to come up with your possible discourse. I'll go to what's essential, *The Symposium* serving you, like all the philosophical objects you have used in your work, only as a transcendental guide (I mean transcendental not in the sense of the illusion about itself that every transcendental philosophy develops when it describes itself as such but in the sense in which it happens that it *misconstrues* what it is when it acknowledges that it needs a guide—the Newtonian physical object, or the Husserlian "percept," or the Heideggerian *Umwelt* of *Sein und Zeit*—when it happens, in the specific form of philosophical misperception, the ideological, that it misconstrues what it is actually in the process of doing, to the extent that it takes its philosophical imaginary for the philosophical symbolic itself, and in that recognition-miscognition it masks its own condition to itself, which is to be structured by entirely other structures than the ones it tranquilly develops, as though it were a matter of those of a transcendental subject—a subject!! You know these confusions from experience, and concerning another object, you have elaborated, in a stage whisper, their theory.) I will thus go to the essential. And in two words.

The desire of the analyst. It sends us to the desire of the analyzed. Desire of a desire. Dual structure of fascination, whence so many interminable-unterminated analyses.

Dual structure of fascination, which, like all dual structures of fascination, produces the imaginary it needs to support that fate, that is, not to emerge from it—fear is always a precious adviser, isn't it? That imaginary can itself be treated like a signifier. And one can also make a discourse out of it, which will have the formal structure of a discourse instead of being a simple rehash of phantasms—a discourse, with the small difference that it will be, in *La Psychanalyse d'aujourd'hui* [*Contemporary Psychoanalysis*] in two volumes at the Presses Universitaires de France, a discourse of the imaginary and not a discourse on the imaginary (that too is conducted at the press, the admirable house! but, note well, in a different collection). You know, you have said it so well: there are, in this order, discourses that are only rehashes and discourses that offer themselves as such, on the condition of fabricating for themselves (an operation that is not at all imaginary but quite an object of reflection, of conscious reflection, the imaginary having total and entire right to the category *consciousness*, which is the philosophical category no. 1 of the philosophical imaginary, an imaginary that is perfectly *conscious*, by which I mean deliberate), in a purely artificial manner (a very objective technique, not at all imaginary, any more than the fabrication technique of the imaginary of *Paris Match,* since it is purely and cynically a deliberate production of the imaginary, is imaginary), on the condition then of fabricating for themselves, in a purely (and consciously) artificial manner, the small technical supplements necessary for a discourse to hold up, the small extensions necessary for it not to be too short: a few concepts, such as object relations, concerning which you have said for all time what needs to be said, that is, very little. But one had to know a devilish lot to say that little, which is unfortunately more dangerous in real life and analytic practice than one might be allowed to hope if one is unaware of the ravages of the ideological *nil,* socially indispensable to its authors, from the objective observation that one was dealing with a void: theoretical nothingness, I mean. But nature has less horror of a vacuum than does ideology, which is no more than the fullness of that void, that fullness overflowing to the point of today submerging our world, no more overflowing than in former times; between those times and today, however, there is this difference, which is that we are, as witnesses and contemporaries of that overflow, the only ones to be committed (or requested or begged) (that is, who are *not* committed or requested or begged, history not having among its official employments either theoretical censors, auctioneers, or public criers [the cry!] [the public cry!] to commit, request, or beg us)—thus by the very necessity that is our law, by virtue of that condition of human historical postmaturation that we can never be our own grandfathers and of the human historical nonprematuration that unfortunately forbids us from being our own grandsons, we are then the only ones obliged, if the fancy takes us, yes, to "have to" make of our bodies a dike for that overflow.

And even then one still has to *know* what is overflowing.

That dual structure of fascination has the result that the desire of desire (analyst-analyzed) can play interminably in a whirligig (before Sartre, who plainly loves carousel horses, or the entrances of the Musée de l'Homme—I won't make him say so, if I may say so—we would have said *in this circle*), in sum, in that "philosophical" circle of intersubjectivity, in which Ricoeur (carousel horses are not the only things in the world for giving an idea of vertigo) finds the wherewithal to satisfy (satisfy: a category of the imaginary; is my terminology precise?)

his legitimate demands (philosophically legitimate) (I cannot touch on his own personal imaginary, having no credentials for doing so and not having, on condition of not reading him too closely, the means). But you have taught us that the imaginary is also nothing but a mimicry of the symbolic, that it bears its mark, but that never is a *mark* on metal—above all in the world of historical deception of a class economy, which is epitomized in the *thing* that is a coin—worth a *title*. The mark comes from *elsewhere*, from that elsewhere which is the Other, which is the name of the Elsewhere, the name of the absolute Outside, the absolute condition of possibility of any inside, even if, as with the nickel of our five centimes, it is false. The absolute condition of possibility of that falsity's existence, of its quality as false, and of its very structure, which allows it to be given and treated as true, if need be by *believing* it to be true (which is not absolutely necessary when one emerges from the analytic object) (one can be conscious and cynical: history is consciousness and cynicism—I mean moral conscience, which is but the good conscience of the cynicism of some and of deception consented to by the others).

The desire of the analyst is *marked*, like every desire, as is *marked* (sealed) the dual relation of Imaginary fascination (I propose a capital I), which renders the circle desire-of-desire specific to the analytic relation, in which the analyst *lives* the very truth of his analyst's desire.

I do not speak, any more than you do, then, of that other dual relation in which the fate of analytic practice is played out; that other dual relation is the dual relation that the patient's desire, marked by the imaginary, attempts to establish between himself and the analyst, a dual relation into which the analyst, precisely, who "isn't playing the game," refuses to enter, because that's why he's an analyst, that is, in order to get his neurotic to move from the imaginary to the symbolic through the vicissitudes of a this time well-scanned Oedipus complex. I am speaking of another dual relation, of the one established by the analyst's desire, of the one that is established by the desire of the analyst: an entirely different situation, one quite strange to the analyst in the street, who, working all week but never on Sunday (pardon), is and always remains more or less in this respect a Sunday analyst. That situation establishes another Imaginary (capital I) at the heart of which the analysis of the patient's imaginary (small i) is developed, that is, most of the time, an analysis that fails, that is interrupted, that one starts afresh with a third party, who in turn starts afresh with the business of the imaginary, and things continue like that until one is fed up or says, "that's enough like that," as of a certain age, or one has been suffi- ciently "improved [*amelioré*]" (the word reeks of chicory [*chicorée*]!) to be able to say hello to daddy mommy or to get married according to the rules, since, after all, gotta make them happy and make children for France! In brief—I say brief because it's not brief, it's very long, it's even interminable, can it even end? analysis terminable-intermin- able—don't you think that the difficulty of translating Freud's words has to do with something completely different from a pure matter of signifiers, I mean of the signifiers officially registered as such and in- ventoried in that admirable system with neither jolts, self-regulator, nor revolutions for which a Genevan (what daring for a Swiss! but a love of social stability can supply illumination concerning the stability of a system in general) one day elaborated the theory, I mean in a dic- tionary. (And the translators' dictionaries, and the etymological ones that give so many peasant joys to Heidegger, who never would have taken the *Holzwege* for paths if he had only been a woodcutter—and he is a philologist a bit in the way he is a woodcutter, treating himself to the sylvan joys of a city-dweller, that is, of a Sunday woodcutter, just as he treats himself to the philological joys of a philosopher, that is, of a Sunday philologist.) (Prévert, who abounds in slyness, rightly says that "Sunday it's the only thing that's true," that is, false). In brief (once again, I repeat my offense), things continue like that for a long time, and at bottom there's no reason for them to stop. A Sunday analyst never truly finishes his analysis. *His* analysis. Of course! The one he's conducting: that of the patient . . . no; *his* analysis, *his own*, even while officially, social-securitily, Delay-psychiatracademically "finishing" his analysis, that of his patient (patience), even when he "finishes" the analysis of his patient.

For concerning that dual relation that he establishes, he himself, through the Imaginary of his analyst's desire, I am not sure that it is ever involved in the analysis of the other imaginary, the one that the desire of the analyzed attempts in vain to establish. And for good rea- son, since to my knowledge (but it could nevertheless happen, for a priori there is no radical obstacle) the patient in analysis is not charged by the society—I mean the Société Psychanalytique de Paris, France, or the International of London—to lead to the threshold of the sym- bolic the imaginary within which the analyst's desire *lives* the *objective* imaginary of the dual situation that is quite simply his *professional con-*

dition, since one cannot decently ask an analyst who occasionally has enough trouble dealing with the imaginary of the patient to self-analyze himself as an analyst (all the same, did not Freud do something that, at a distance, resembled that?), that is, to deal with his own Imaginary, well, things continue.

I am saying that you are at the very point where everything will be played out. At the point where the desire of the analyst (ah! those damned countertransferences . . .) will reveal to us through your theoretical work what *mark* is carried, beneath the legal stamp of every mark *überhaupt*, which is the mark of the symbolic in general, by the Imaginary of the analyst.

There are good reasons to bet that this mark bears some famous names, among which Paris, London, the provinces, and a few wives will be involved. For as you say, it happens that analysts are married. And as you know in your flesh, they have businesses at good addresses, arms longer than their sleeves, an official place under the sun of our bourgeois society, their books sell, and—does one ever know?—one has to *think of the future*.

The future: they can certainly think about it. They're right. There will be revolutions that will be more bitter and cruel to them than the one inspired by their fear of losing their social position, their income, and the rest. One can always escape the financial and social effects of a social revolution. And it's not worth it (God save them!), crossing the sea . . . it's enough to give a deposit, a guarantee, in short, to know how to *conduct oneself*. In that respect, they have only to continue. They have, dare I say, what it takes. No, I am speaking of a different revolution, the one you are preparing without them knowing it, the one from which no sea in the world will ever be able to protect them, and no respectability, whether capitalist or socialist, the one that will strip them of the security of their *Imaginary* and that will one day give them the possibility (they will then be able to freely choose their destiny, without needing social or political guarantees) of delivering their human desire, which has no name, not the name of man, and without doubt not the name of desire (man being, as poor Feuerbach used to say quite unconsciously, the name of all names, just as God was formerly the name of all names, which makes him strictly speaking superfluous, except for those who need that label to sell under it an entirely different —and unconfessable—product) (desire being *the name [nom] of every no [non]*, that is, of every *yes*, which renders it strictly speaking superfluous when an analysis *is finished*—but when is it these days?—which will render it strictly speaking superfluous when the analysis of analysts will be possible, finished, and their analyses—that of their patient patients—finished . . .), that revolution which will one day give them the possibility of delivering their "man's" "desire" from the Imaginary of the social, religious, moral, matrimonial, etc. condition of the analytic profession in which it lies literally bewitched.

They do well to be afraid of that revolution. Just as a neurotic may be afraid of knocking at the door of an analyst, however duly certified. Afraid of the revolution that can make them men like others. Afraid? The best—even the good ones, who are legion—don't merit that fear.

For like all true revolutions, it does nothing but utter a different word that must still be uttered (as we utter the word *desire*) and that a man wrote, in an unfortunate time, on walls and in notebooks, but whose object it is to render the very use of that word superfluous: freedom.

Yours

[Louis Althusser]

6. Jacques Lacan to Louis Althusser

This Monday, 1-6-64

Dear Althusser,

I preferred not to run the risks of the Italian mail—and during these holidays—and toward a rather remote spot, I believe—for my wishes to reach you.

I myself am leaving today for six days in Rome (Enrico Castelli[16] Colloquium; do you know that extraordinary individual[?] German theologian + Ricoeur + Waelhens + etc. around: technique, casuistry, and eschatology [*sic*].) Well, it's madness, but I hope to relax there.

Here is my card.

With the same hand, I am sending an invitation for M. Flacelière,[17] but there is a secretary, I believe. Would you tell my wife her name—in order to invite her as well?

Believe me your

Lacan

7. Jacques Lacan to Louis Althusser

This Wednesday, 1-22-64

Rather good, your fellow.[18]

Thanks.

J.L.

8. Jacques Lacan to Louis Althusser[19]

[Thessalonica] This 31-III-64

Dear Althusser,

This photo comes from Pater Photios—the most hospitable of men—after you. To be sure.

The cell he occupies is in Kariès, the principal town of this peninsula, where monks feel at home and which is called the Holy Mountain.

There are things to be said about it, and the excursion tears you away from the present.

Believe me your

J. Lacan

9. Jacques Lacan to Louis Althusser

This Monday, 6-VII-64

Dear Althusser,

The other evening I telephoned you for this bit of information—in reaction to my astonishment that one might have an answer for which I thought I had addressed the most reliable (or informed) sources.

I decided not to satisfy myself with the telephone to tell you how grateful I am for your article.[20] Profound and relevant: adding the dimension of your own meditation on the subject.

I am quite honored by such an effort and comforted by its utter success.

Believe me your very faithful

J. Lacan

10. Jacques Lacan to Louis Althusser

This 19-X-65

My dear Althusser,

I am in the process of reading the volume you were good enough to send to me, with delectation.[21]

You may have gotten wind of the visit I paid to the director of the Ecole. An annual visit I had not been able to make at the end of the school year.

I did not have time that day to knock on your door.

I would like to be sure that someday, doing so, I would not be disturbing you.

Your

Lacan

11. Louis Althusser to Jacques Lacan

[Paris], 11-7-66[22]

Dear Lacan,

On the question that concerns you, and that concerns us, you will find a few very rudimentary and poorly elaborated elements, which are at most *indicative* of the problem, at least of its existence, in

(1) *Lire "Le Capital"* [*Reading "Capital"*] volume 1, preface.

I don't dare suggest that you read the entire preface. I attempted there to indicate the necessity of a theory of *reading* on the basis of the very particular reading Marx does of the texts of his predecessors (the classical economists), which I have called, precisely, a "symptomal reading," proposing a frightful neologism (I hesitated for a long time before that grammatical barbarism, which seemed theoretically necessary to me). See pp. 1–40.

This theory of symptomal reading indicates its conditions of possibility in the *nature* of the discourse underpinning its act of *reading*: a theoretical discourse, whether it be palpably ideological (the economists) or *already* scientific (Marx). (This science-ideology distinction is to be handled with the greatest caution, but *provisionally*, while waiting for a more serious analysis, on which I am presently working, it performs some objective services, whose effects, to be sure, will need to be rectified.) The *nature* of this discourse seems to me able to be fixed by the *theoretical problematic* sustaining it. Behind that theoretical problematic a *reality* that is its determined condition is outlined: the existing *theoretical conjuncture* and its (articulated) relations with the *historical* conjuncture in the broad sense. The concept of conjuncture refers in turn to the concept of *history*.

On the concept of conjuncture and the concept of history, see *Lire "Le Capital,"* preface (in truth, the entire end of the preface constantly alludes to it), and also volume 2 (*L'Objet du "Capital"*: 4, 5, 6, 9).

See as well the text by *Balibar* in volume 2: it is (in its entirety) of the very first importance. It is there that one can already see clearly enough in what ways the Marxist concept of structure can be distinguished without any possible confusion from the Lévi-Straussian concept of structure (and all the more from all the idealist aberrations of the "structuralists"), precisely because the Lévi-Straussian concept of structure is *theoretically* ambiguous. (It oscillates between a subjectivist conception and a Platonic conception of structure, between structure as intention and structure as *eidos*. The locus of that ambiguity can be assigned in his case with precision: it is his completely aberrant conception of the *unconscious*.) One should not make a mistake about the term *subjectivist* temptation (*intention*) in the Lévi-Straussian conception of structure: it is a matter of social subjectivity, social "intention." I am alluding to the fact that the unconscious of the structure for Lévi-Strauss is an "unconscious" social intention (that is, an "unintentional" one, as Godelier says with marvelous naïveté), one that expresses the society's *will to live*. I am using words that are so many metaphors, but you will understand me. Ultimately structure is unconscious in Lévi-Strauss, and it is a structure "*so that it* (society) can live." It's in that "so that" of the telos (to live) of society that the temptation of conceiving of structure as *intention* and subjectivity is concealed (that is, revealed).

To be sure, one can criticize Lévi-Strauss on other scores, but it is there, at that precise point, from my point of view, that *one cannot not take one's distance from him*. And it is, I believe, very important for analysis as well to be well aware that one cannot, properly speaking, speak of a social *unconscious*; otherwise, all confusions are permitted (including those that may haunt, if not the texts of Freud you alluded to last night—since I don't know them, I can't speak of them—at least their reading).

It is at bottom for that reason of principle that I said to you that, seen from the outside, and, I admit, from a certain distance, your theoretical relations with Lévi-Strauss may today, *to a certain extent*, be a problem for us if they are not clarified. Everyone (you know who) has an interest in confusing you, under the term of structuralism, with Lévi-Strauss. *Not us.* And I believe that neither do you have any interest in letting that confusion occur, even independently of yourself, even at a great distance from yourself (and you are aware that it occurs as well in individuals who have *declared themselves* to be very close to you).

I am sending you under the same cover a very schematic and very crude talk that I gave two weeks ago at the Ecole.[23] Should you read it, consider it as no more than a "symptom," but a symptom that is . . . insofar as is possible, *conscious!* (in which case it would no longer be *only* a symptom . . .)

I was happy to see you again. I offer you my fond best wishes for your vacation and for your work. For us, it is very important that you exist, that you are the theoretician that you are, and that you pursue your vanguard work. You are not alone. The front is vast, and there are, or there are beginning to be, many other combatants, even if they are not all fighting on the same line, at the same point, or under the same "flag" and even if you have reason to believe *certain* of them (I don't say all) at present far from you.

I convey to you my intense and lucid friendship,

[Louis Althusser]

12. Jacques Lacan to Louis Althusser

[Paris]

Friday, before leaving for the hospital,
consequently, in a hurry

Dear Althusser,

I don't want to bother you on the telephone. But be apprised that there is no need for you to trouble yourself with finding me a new shelter. (I was with Nassif, as I ought to have been, but don't take that into account).

I shall not go anywhere else, moreover—and here I shall vacate the premises promptly.[24]

The letter I have received happily brings into relief the incidence of the "reform." Informing the students of it as well as of my actual position in the university will perhaps leave a slightly durable trace in their heads.

They tell me (it's a way of speaking) that I am the only (!) lecture course that is absolutely not being contested: this intervention and its sequels will thus assume its value.

For more details, I'll see you on Thursday. But by then the question will already be quashed. The end of the trimester is quite favorable to it.

Your

J. L.

Notes

Introduction

1. The Althusser collection of IMEC contains abundant archives concerning the seminar. Louis Althusser himself delivered two lectures there, of which a record survives, one in the form of a frequently erroneous transcription and the other in an almost complete recording. A separate edition of those two lectures is currently being prepared.

2. Cf. Elisabeth Roudinesco, *La Bataille de cent ans: Histoire de la psychanalyse en France*, 2 vols. (Paris: Seuil, 1986), vol. 2 (English translation by Jeffrey Mehlman, *Jacques Lacan & Co.: A History of Psychoanalysis in France, 1925–1986* [Chicago: University of Chicago Press, 1990]); and *Jacques Lacan: Esquisse d'une vie, histoire d'un système de pensée* (Paris: Fayard, 1993), in which the author devotes a chapter to Lacan's "Dialogue with Louis Althusser."

3. Concerning Franca, who was the Italian translator of *Pour Marx*, see Louis Althusser, *L'Avenir dure longtemps* (Paris: Stock/IMEC), 133 (English translation by R. Veasey, *The Future Lasts Forever* [London: Chatto and Windus, 1993]). The correspondence used in this volume is drawn from a collection of more than 300 letters sent by Louis Althusser to Franca from 1961 to 1972. We owe our access to them to Yann Moulier-Boutang.

4. See in this volume Althusser's letters to Lacan of December 4 and 10, 1963.

5. Jean-Pierre Lefebvre, preface to G. F. Hegel, *Phénoménologie de l'esprit* (Paris: Aubier, 1991), 11.

Translator's Notes

* Neither "Three Notes on the Theory of Discourses" nor "On Transference and Countertransference" has been included in this volume. See translator's preface.

** This edition in English does not include these variants.

1. Freud and Lacan: Introduction

1. *Pour Marx* (Paris: Maspero, 1965), 67 (English translation by Ben Brewster, *For Marx* [New York: Vintage, 1970]).

2. This text has been published (jointly by Stock and IMEC) in the first volume of *Ecrits philosophiques et politiques de Louis Althusser* (Paris: IMEC, 1994).

3. See his correspondence with Lacan in this collection.

4. Louis Althusser, *L'Avenir dure longtemps* (Paris: Stock/IMEC), 124–25 (English translation by R. Veasey, *The Future Lasts Forever* [London: Chatto and Windus, 1993]).

5. "La psychanalyse, idéologie réactionnaire," *La Nouvelle Critique* 7 (June 1949): 52–73, reproduced in *La Scission de 1953*, supplement to *Ornicar?* 7 (1976). Louis Althusser quite probably read the article when it appeared. A copy annotated in his hand has been found in his library.

6. *Positions* (Paris: Editions Sociales, 1976).

7. He was probably referring to the first of his "Trois notes sur la théorie des discours."

Freud and Lacan

1. Cf. "Philosophie et sciences humaines," *Revue de l'enseignement philosophique* 5 (June–July 1963): 7 and 11, n. 14: "Marx based his theory on the rejection of the myth of 'homo economicus'; Freud based his theory on the rejection of the myth of 'homo psychologicus.' Lacan has seen and understood Freud's liberating break. He has understood it in the full sense of the word, taking it in the literality of its rigor and forcing it to produce, without concession or compromise, its full consequences. Like anyone else, he may err in details—indeed, in the choice of his philosophical bearings—but we owe him the *essential*."

2. The most threatening temptations are represented by *philosophy* (which deliberately reduces all psychoanalysis to the dual experience of therapy and finds in it the wherewithal to "verify" the themes of phenomenological intersubjectivity, existence as project, or more generally, personalism); by psychology, which annexes most of the categories of psychoanalysis as so many attributes of the "subject," which plainly is not a category that it finds at all troubling; finally, by sociology, which, coming to the assistance of psychology, supplies the wherewithal to give the "reality principle" its objective content (social and familial imperatives), which the "subject" has but to "internalize" to be armed with a "superego" and its corresponding categories. Subordinated in that manner to psychology and sociology, psychoanalysis is most often reduced to a technique of "emotional" or "affective" readaptation, to a retraining of the "relational function," neither of which has anything to do with its real object—but both of which unfortunately respond to a strong and

(in addition) highly tendentious demand in the contemporary world. It is as a result of that bias that psychoanalysis has become a common object of consumption in culture (i.e., ideology).

3. These are the two German expressions, made famous by Freud, with which a small child he was observing designated the appearance and disappearance of his mother through the manipulation of a commonplace object that "represented" her: "here!" "gone!" It was a spool.

4. *Formally*. For the Law of Culture, whose first form is language, is not exhausted by language; it has as contents actual kinship structures and the determined ideological formations through which the individuals inscribed in those structures live their function. It is not enough to know that the Western family is patriarchal and exogamous (kinship structure); one also must elucidate the ideological formations that govern conjugality, paternity, maternity, and childhood: what is it "to be a husband," "to be a father," "to be a mother" in our present world? A great deal of investigation remains to be accomplished concerning those specific ideological formations.

5. A certain neurobiology and a certain psychology were quite gratified to discover in Freud a theory of "stages" that they did not hesitate to translate directly and exhaustively into a theory of (either neurobiological or bioneuropsychological) "phased maturation"—mechanically attributing to neurobiological maturation the role of an "essence" of which the Freudian "stages" would be the pure and simple "phenomena." This perspective is but a reissuing of the old mechanist parallelism.

6. One would risk misconstruing the theoretical bearing of that formal condition if one opposed to it the biological appearance of the concepts (libido, affects, drives, desire) in which Freud thought the "content" of the unconscious—for example, when he says that the dream is the "plenitude of desire" (*Wunscherfüllung*). It is in the same manner that Lacan wants to bring man back to the "language of his unconscious desire." It is, however, on the basis of that formal condition that these (apparently biological) concepts take on their authentic meaning, that this meaning can be assigned and thought, and that a technique of therapy can be defined and applied. Desire, a fundamental category of the unconscious, is understandable in its specificity only as the idiosyncratic meaning of the discourse of the human subject's unconscious: the meaning that emerges in and through the "play" of the signifying chain of which the discourse of the unconscious is composed. As such, "desire" is marked by the structure that commands human development. As such, desire is radically distinct from organic "need," which is biological in essence. Between organic need and unconscious desire, there is no essential continuity—any more than there exists an essential continuity between the biological existence of man and his historical existence. Desire is determined in its equivocal being (its lack in being, Lacan says) by the structure of the order imposing on it its mark and consigning it to an existence without place, the

existence of repression, to its resources and its disappointments. One does not gain access to the specific reality of desire by starting from organic need, any more than one gains access to the specific reality of historical existence by starting from the biological existence of "man." On the contrary, just as it is the categories of history that allow one to define the specificity of the historical existence of man, including such apparently purely biological determinations as his "needs" or demographic phenomena, by distinguishing his historical existence from a purely biological existence, so the essential categories of the unconscious are what allow one to apprehend and define the very meaning of desire by distinguishing it from the biological realities underlying it (exactly as biological existence underlies and supports historical existence) but without either *constituting* it or *determining* it.

7. Lacan's expressions ("machine"), adapting Freud (*"ein anderes Schauspiel . . . Schauplatz"*). From Politzer, who speaks of "drama," to Freud and Lacan, who speak of theater, stage, staging, machinery, the theatrical genre, director, and so on, there is all the distance separating the spectator, who takes himself for the theater, from the theater itself.

8. If one understands the term *effect* in the context of a classical theory of causality, one will think it in terms of the actual presence of the cause in its effect (cf. Spinoza).

9. Bibliographical study note: Lacan's work, which is at present dispersed in numerous collective publications, can be approached most easily in the following order:

1. "Les Complexes familiaux en pathologie," in *La Vie mentale,* vol. 8 of *Encyclopédie française,* ed. de Monzie (Paris: Larousse, 1938).

2. "La Causalité psychique" in L. Bonnaté, H. Ey, et al., *Le Problème de la psychogenèse des névroses et des psychoses* (Desclée de Brouwer, 1950), 123–65.

3. "Le Stade du miroir comme formateur de la fonction du jeu," *Revue française de psychanalyse* 13, no. 4 (1949): 449–55.

4. "La Chose freudienne," *Evolution psychiatrique* 1 (1956): 225–52.

5. "Les Formations de l'inconscient (Seminar 57–58)," *Bulletin de psychologie* 11 (1957–58): 4–5; 12 (1958–59): 2–4.

6. "Les Relations d'objet et les structures freudiennes (Seminar 56–57)," *Bulletin de psychologie* 10 (1956–57): 7, 10, 12, 14.

7. "Le Désir et son interprétation (Seminar 58–59)," *Bulletin de psychologie* 13 (Jan. 1959–60): 5–6.

8. The seven issues of the journal *La Psychanalyse* (PUF) and in particular Lacan's presentation and interventions at the Rome Congress (vol. 1 [1956]: 81–166) (Lacan's presentation: "La Parole et le langage en psychanalyse").

The two texts in no. 6 ("Remarques sur le rapport de D. Lagache: La Direction de la cure" [1961]: 111–47).

The text in no. 3 ("L'Instance de la lettre dans l'inconscient" [1957]: 47–81).

The text in no. 6 ("Sur les psychoses"), etc.

9. Among the texts published by students of Lacan or influenced by his teaching, the reader is advised to start with S. Leclaire's articles in *La Psychanalyse*; the article by S. Leclaire and J. Laplanche on the unconscious (*Temps modernes*, July 1961); J.-B. Lefèvre-Pontalis's articles on Freud today (*Temps modernes*, nos. 124, 125, 126 [1956]); J. Laplanche's work on Hölderlin (*Hölderlin et la question du père* [Paris: PUF, 1961]); Maud Mannoni's book *L'Enfant arriéré et sa mère* (Paris: Seuil, 1964) (English translation by A. M. Sheridan Smith, *The Backward Child and His Mother* [New York: Pantheon, 1972]).

2. Letters to D.: INTRODUCTION

1. Louis Althusser, *L'Avenir dure longtemps* (Paris: Stock/IMEC), 64 (English translation by R. Veasey, *The Future Lasts Forever* [London: Chatto and Windus, 1993]).

2. "Louis Althusser's two texts are quite interesting and are entirely deserving of publication," René Diatkine has written to us, adding, "Mine, on the other hand, was not written to be published; it was composed in circumstances that you can imagine. I can thus only be opposed to its publication, all the more so in that it no longer corresponds to my current way of thinking."

Letters to D.

1. The precise quotation is "but who can identify with a sauce?" in R. Diatkine, "Agressivité et fantasme d'agression," *Revue française de psychanalyse* 30 (1960): 71.

2. "As adults, we are wounded in our dignity as men when we learn the truth about certain colonial regimes, about Auschwitz, or about Hiroshima. Our good conscience as bourgeois liberals allows us quickly to forget those unbearable realities, unless our masochism as left-wing intellectuals plunges us back into them. But it is more convenient for us to find aggressiveness bestial." Ibid., 69.

3. Sacha Nacht was at the time president of the Société Psychanalytique de Paris, of which René Diatkine was a member.

4. R. Diatkine, "Agressivité et fantasme d'agression," 46.

5. For example, in the "Note complémentaire sur l'humanisme réel," republished in *Pour Marx*, 253–58 (Paris: Maspero, 1965), 255 (English translation by Ben Brewster, *For Marx* [New York: Vintage, 1970]).

6. R. Diatkine, "Agressivité et fantasme d'agression," 77–79.

7. Ibid., 75.

8. R. Diatkine and S. Lebovici, "Etude des fantasmes chez l'enfant," *Revue française de psychanalyse* 18, no. 1 (1954): 108–55.

9. Ibid.

10. Louis Althusser appears to be referring to the following formula of Lacan's: "The death instinct expresses essentially the limit of the historical function of the subject; that limit is death, not as the ultimate expiration of the individual's life, nor as the empirical certitude of the subject, but according to the formula given by Heidegger for it, as 'the absolutely idiosyncratic, unconditional, unsurpassable, certain, and, as such, undetermined possibility of the subject,' by which we understand the subject defined by its historicity." This passage from the "Rome Discourse," republished in *Ecrits* (Paris: Seuil, 1966), 318, is underscored by Althusser in the issue (no. 1) of *La Psychanalyse* (where it was first published) found in his library.

11. See, for example, [Nicolas de] Malebranche, *Entretiens sur la Métaphysique et sur la Religion* (Paris:Vrin, 1947), x, 2, and 4.

12. A part of the sentence appears to have disappeared during typing, making it difficult to understand this passage.

3. The Tbilisi Affair: INTRODUCTION

1. Léon Chertok regularly sent him his offprints with friendly dedications.

2. It is unfortunately not possible to quote or even summarize those criticisms here, but the texts, it should be recalled, are available for consultation in the Althusser collection of IMEC.

3. *The Unconscious, Nature, Function, Methods of Study*, 3 vols. (Tbilisi: Metsniereba, 1978). Louis Althusser's text appeared in the first volume, 239–53.

4. In Louis Althusser, *Ideologie und ideologische Staatsapparat* (Hamburg: VSA, 1977), 89–107.

5. In Louis Althusser, *Nuevos Escritos* (Barcelona: Laia, 1978), 107–35.

6. Between three and four hundred copies, according to a letter of April 26, 1984, from Yves Suaudeau, the editor-in-chief of Editions Privat, to Louis Althusser.

7. Catherine Clément, "Ephémérides, XVIII," *L'Ane*, no. 18 (September–October 1984): 24.

8. Letter of April 20, 1984, from Louis Althusser to Yves Suaudeau.

9. "This is the first time that his voice has come back to us. It will have been thanks to a spoliation," Catherine Clément would note in *L'Ane*.

10. We owe the mention of this slip to Bernard Doray—one of the authors of *Dialogues franco-soviétiques sur la psychanalyse*—who had indicated it to Léon Chertok in a letter of protest that he had sent to him following this "affair" and a copy of which he had transmitted to Althusser.

The Discovery of Dr. Freud

1. In the corrected version, after reading the criticisms that Elisabeth Roudinesco sent him and that we are publishing here, Louis Althusser replaced the expression "effects of the unconscious" by "manifestations of the unconscious" in the first two of his "remarks" but did not subsequently effect this change in the rest of his text.

2. "The conscious" in place of "consciousness."

3. "The unconscious manifests itself" in place of "the effects of the unconscious manifest themselves."

4. See our introduction to this chapter.

On Marx and Freud

1. This entire paragraph disappeared from the edition of the proceedings of the Tbilisi colloquium published in 1978.

2. In the version of this text that he had transmitted to the German publisher VSA in January 1977, Althusser had mentioned that this whole paragraph could be cut. This paragraph does not appear in the edition of the proceedings of the Tbilisi colloquium, without it being possible to ascertain whether the same freedom to retain (or not) this paragraph had been granted to the Soviet publishers or whether they had themselves, as we have previously seen, taken the liberty of making the cut.

4. "In the Name of the Analysands . . .": Introduction

1. Questioned on the subject, Jacques-Alain Miller provided us with the following written testimony: "The room of the PLM, flat, without a platform, two lines of chairs. Lacan at the table serving as rostrum. I am seated in the left section, in the first row; there is an empty seat at my left. I feel something like a breeze; someone has just rushed to my side. I turn—it's Althusser. I haven't seen him in years. We speak to each other. He is in a state of agitation I have never seen him in. I suggest that he go with me to the rear of the room, listen to his comments, try to calm him. He gets up and takes the floor. I find him at the exit. He is going to write; I will drop by to see him on Monday.

"Monday, in his office, rue d'Ulm. He has me read a typed text that he has just written and wants to publish; he asks me my opinion. I answer him that if he 'trusts me,' he won't publish the text, and will keep it in his archives: it is not at the 'level' of what he succeeded in writing in the past. He informs me that he is to give an interview to *Le Monde* in the afternoon; I advise him against it. We speak for an hour. He appears to have accepted my suggestions.

"The next day, I call, come upon Hélène, and tell her that I found Althusser in very bad shape. She answers dryly that I have only to tell him so, that she has nothing to do with it, and that he is under treatment" (July 21, 1993).

2. Louis Althusser, *L'Avenir dure longtemps* (Paris: Stock/IMEC), 180 (English translation by R. Veasey, *The Future Lasts Forever* [London: Chatto and Windus, 1993]).

Open Letter to Analysands and Analysts

1. Althusser is alluding to a tract titled "Colle d'école," signed by Jacques Rudraf, distributed in the course of the meeting, and on whose reverse side he took notes completing those on a page of his appointment book, reproduced on page 126.

2. Althusser is undoubtedly alluding to the incident related by C. Clément in *Le Matin* (March 17, 1980) when, interrupting him from the rostrum, the psychoanalyst Anne-Lise Stern said to him, "One may wonder on which couch *you* are in order to speak as you do," after Althusser had said, "One would think that you had subordinated your analysands to your own worries" (see the subsequent text).

3. "Ce qui ne peut plus durer dans le parti communiste," three articles that appeared in *Le Monde* on April 25, 26, and 27, 1978, and were later incorporated in the volume of the same name published by Maspero that same year.

4. Uncompleted text.

5. See L. Althusser, *Journal de captivité: Stalag XA 1940–1945* (Paris: Stock/IMEC, 1992).

5. Correspondence with Jacques Lacan: Introduction

1. Cf. Elisabeth Roudinesco, *La Bataille de cent ans: Histoire de la psychanalyse en France,* 2 vols. (Paris: Seuil, 1986), vol. 2 (English translation by Jeffrey Mehlman, *Jacques Lacan & Co.* [Chicago: University of Chicago Press, 1990]).

2. Cf. Jacques Lacan, *Séminaire XI: Les Quatre Concepts fondamentaux de la psychanalyse* (Paris: Seuil, 1973).

Correspondence with Jacques Lacan

1. Lecture delivered in 1945, which Althusser undoubtedly did not attend. Cf. Yann Moulier-Boutang, *Louis Althusser: Une Biographie* (Paris: Grasset, 1992), 303.

2. Reference is to the article "Philosophie et sciences humaines," *Revue de l'enseignement philosophique* 5 (June–July, 1963), in which Althusser specifies in a note that Lacan "has seen and understood Freud's liberating break" and that as a result, "one owes him *the essential.*" See on this subject Althusser's reminder

of that brief mention at the beginning of his article "Freud and Lacan."

3. See the introduction to this volume.

4. Louis Althusser is referring to his seminar on psychoanalysis of 1963–64. See the introduction to this volume.

5. Robert Flacelière had just been named director of the Ecole Normale Supérieure.

6. Jean Prigent.

7. Reference is to the article "Sur la dialectique matérialiste," *La Pensée* 110 (August 1963): 5–46.

8. Ibid.

9. Jacques Lacan and Louis Althusser had met for the first time the previous evening and had dined together.

10. Althusser had originally typed "the only ones" (*les seuls*) and then eliminated the plural.

11. Cf. *Temps modernes* (1961): 184–85, a special issue devoted to Maurice Merleau-Ponty, with articles by Jean Hyppolite, Jacques Lacan, Claude Lefort, Jean-Bertrand Pontalis, Jean-Paul Sartre, Alphonse de Waelhens, and Jean Wahl.

12. In all probability the reference is to the colloquium "The Unconscious" held at Bonneval from October 30 to November 2, 1960, in the course of which Paul Ricoeur intervened. Concerning the episode, see E. Roudinesco, *La Bataille de cent ans*, 2:317–28.

13. This letter was not sent; see our introduction to the correspondence. Note the existence of an anonymous, incomplete, and often erroneous transcription of a recording by Louis Althusser on December 8, 1963, on "the end of analysis," that was found in his archives.

14. Louis Althusser is probably referring to his preceding letter of December 4.

15. Cf. Jacques Lacan, *Séminaire VIII: Le Transfert* (Paris: Seuil, 1991).

16. Enrico Castelli, an Italian theologian, was the organizer of a colloquium held in Rome from January 7 to January 12, 1964, on the subject "technique and casuistry." A summary of Lacan's interventions at that colloquium appeared under the title "Du *Trieb* de Freud et du désir du psychanalyste," in *Ecrits* (Paris: Seuil, 1966), 851–54. On the encounter between Paul Ricoeur and Lacan on the occasion of that colloquium, see E. Roudinesco, *La Bataille de cent ans*, 2:398–405.

17. Reference is to the director of the Ecole Normale Supérieure.

18. Reference is to Jacques-Alain Miller, Lacan's future son-in-law and at the time one of Althusser's students. In a letter sent to us, Jacques-Alain Miller indicates that on that day he had just "spoken for the first time in Lacan's seminar and asked him a question about the adjective 'ontological' that he used somewhere to characterize 'lack.' Whence a brief discussion." He specifies, "That very afternoon, I passed by at Althusser's to tell him of the

exploit—and he surprised me by showing the note that Lacan had sent him. Here, a spark fixed something for me."

19. Text written on a black-and-white postcard, sent from Thessalonica (Greece), the reproduction of a portion of a fresco in the monastery representing the archangel Gabriel.

20. Reference is to the article "Freud and Lacan," which Louis Althusser had sent him in a typed version.

21. Reference is to *Pour Marx*, which had just been published by Maspero. Instead of treating it as he had Lacan's other letters, Althusser had placed this one in a folder containing letters from eminent figures or friends, most of them admiring (among whom were Jean-Toussaint Desanti, Jean-François Revel, Georges Canguilhem, François Châtelet, Gilles Deleuze, Pierre Bourdieu, Michel Foucault, Roland Barthes, and Jean-Pierre Vernant), after the book's publication.

22. In all probability this should read July 13, since, according to his date book, Louis Althusser had an appointment "at Lacan's place, 5 rue de Lille," on Tuesday, July 12, and this letter was clearly written after they had seen each other again, as is said at the end of it.

23. Reference is to the text "Conjoncture philosophique et recherche théorique marxiste,' which appeared posthumously in *Ecrits philosophiques et politiques* (Paris: Stock, 1994).

24. Jacques Lacan would put an end to his seminar "*D'un Autre à l'autre*" (*Séminaire XVI*, unpublished) at the Ecole Normale Supérieure after the session of June 25, 1969.

Index

Index

Index